Lilies

Michael Jefferson-Brown

Special photography
Andrew Lawson

Lilies

A guide to choosing and
growing lilies

RIZZOLI
NEW YORK

Publishing Director Jane O'Shea
Art Director Helen Lewis
Project Editor Carole McGlynn
Art Editor Paul Welti
Photography Andrew Lawson, Sarah Cuttle
Production Beverley Richardson, Vincent Smith

First published in 2003 by Quadrille Publishing Limited

First published in the United States of America in 2004 by
Rizzoli International Publications Inc.
300 Park Avenue South, New York, NY 10010
www.rizzoliusa.com

ISBN 0-8478-2597-3
Library of Congress Catalog Control Number: 2003110080
Printed and bound in China

Half-title (page 1): Oriental hybrid lily of the Orienpet
Group, *Lilium* 'Black Beauty'

Title (pages 2–3): Candidum Group species lily,
Lilium pyrenaicum

This page: Asiatic hybrid lily, *Lilium* 'Lollipop'

Opposite page: Oriental hybrid lily of the Orienpet
Group, *Lilium* 'Catherine the Great'

contents

I admit to an infatuation with all lilies—
I find them both intriguing and exciting. Their
diversity in appearance is allied to a many-
faceted worth in the garden that makes them
an increasingly important ornamental plant.

introducing lilies

Lilies of one kind or another look set to make
the most of the opportunities offered by the
size and form of today's gardens and, with
their drought resistance, to exploit our
apparently changing climate patterns. We shall
be looking at the species to suggest the most
suitable for a variety of sites, while the legion
of hybrids will test our discrimination.

Lilies have always been regarded as something special, as glamorous plants. They have been associated with humankind for millennia, being used both decoratively and as a source of food and of medicine. Some, such as the Madonna lily (*L. candidum*), were used in religious observances in times well before the Christian era.

introducing lilies: history

The Madonna lily (*L. candidum*) has been grown in Europe as a fodder and decorative plant for at least 2,500 years, especially around the Mediterranean. Today it is as much a favorite of modest gardens as of imposing ones.

Once the showy flowers of wild lilies caught the eye of plant hunters, bulbs were collected and sent from their native habitats to those parts of the world where gardens were established. By the sixteenth century there were already several species in cultivation in Europe. The introduction of new species gained momentum as China and other parts of the Far East were more fully explored during the second half of the nineteenth century and the beginning of the twentieth. A number of naturally occurring hybrids had been found in the wild, and more arose under cultivation, but it was not until halfway through the twentieth century that the real hybrid revolution got under way.

These are exciting times for lilies. The new hybrids being bred are often kinds only dreamed of a few decades ago. The huge size of some of the newer Oriental hybrids may cause some slight unease to those of conservative taste but the other fields of breeding activity can be wholeheartedly welcomed. The Asiatics will retain their appeal, but the result of mating these with *L. longiflorum* has produced a hugely robust race of large, showy, garden-worthy stars. In another direction, the influence of the alkalinity-tolerant *L. henryi* in the crossbreeding of Orientals may be the most important long-term advance for gardeners, producing plants that can be grown in soils of widely different pH values but with the opulent beauty of the Orientals.

earliest times

The illustrations are taken from John Parkinson's *Paradisi in Sole Paradisus Terrestris* of 1629, "The Garden of Pleasant Flowers." The flowers, from left to right, are as listed there, with their present-day names in parentheses. 1 Martagon Flore albo. The white Martagon (*L. martagon* var. *album*). 2 Martagon five. *Lilium canadense* maculatum. The spotted Martagon or Lily of Canada (*L. canadense*). 3 Martagon Pomponeum. The Martagon Pompony or early red Martagon (*L. pomponium*).

It is impossible to pinpoint the first time that human culture became closely associated with lilies and to be sure which was the first species so favored, but the joint favorites are the tiger lily (*L. lancifolium*) and the Madonna lily (*L. candidum*). The tiger lily has for thousands of years formed a part of the staple diet in regions of China, where it would appear that various forms have been selected to grow as a fodder crop; perhaps the fairly widespread distribution of the triploid form (having three sets of chromosomes) may be put down to its usefulness and vigor. The native peoples of North America also used many bulbs, including lilies, as food—a practice that presumably stretched back into the mists of antiquity.

The claims for the Madonna lily to be the first one intimately associated with humankind again rest primarily on its use as food, but the flowers were widely linked with religious and civic ceremonial. This lily appears as a decorative motif in a Minoan fresco found at Amnissos, near Knossos on the Greek island of Crete, now housed in the Heraklion Museum. Just when the fresco was made is uncertain, but the Minoan civilization dates as far back as 3000–1500 B.C. Representations of the Madonna lily can also be found in the work of the Assyrians and the early Egyptians. Only later did it become associated with Christianity, as one of many plants grown by monks for their medicinal properties, real or imagined. It was known as a symbol of Saint John the Baptist and of various other saints and was first firmly linked with the Virgin Mary in 1043 in Spain, where the bulbs may have been introduced by the Moors. But it was with the Renaissance that *L. candidum* became the unequivocal symbol for the Mother of Christ—the Madonna lily.

From early on, bulbs of *L. candidum* were spread all over the countries around the Mediterranean and farther afield; the Phoenicians, as the great sailor-traders of early times, have been given credit for much of this dispersal. The original home of the species is now assumed to have been the eastern Mediterranean and the Balkans. Happily, the species proved an amenable one, and by the beginning of the nineteenth century it had become a familiar plant in cottage gardens as well as in those of the large estates. Its success as a cottage garden plant was probably due to being allowed its own undisturbed regime, growing away from other lilies. Its vulnerability to virus diseases has been such that stocks have been weakened and eventually killed when attacked by viruses that have had less effect on other species.

4 Lilium album. The white lily
(*L. candidum*)

INTO GARDENS: EUROPEAN SPECIES

Collections of diverse plants were built up in scholastic and monastic centers, often for their possible medicinal value. Herbals show that several European species were being grown in both institutional and private gardens as early as 1597. The herbal of the botanist John Gerard, dating from this time, lists five kinds— *L. candidum, L. bulbiferum, L. croceum, L. chalcedonicum,* and *L. martagon.* John Parkinson in his *Paradisi in Sole Paradisus Terrestris* of 1629, adds three new kinds—*L. pyrenaicum* and *L. pomponium,* both from European mountain ranges, and *L. canadense,* an early entry from North America.

Of these species it is the Martagon lily that is now the most popular. Earlier herbals showed *L. martagon* to be well established as a garden plant since the fifteenth century. Though it is doubtful whether any medicinal role was found for this lily, its decorative value must have been recognized, since bulbs were spread around all the main European gardens. The Martagons are much prized for their longevity, their graceful long spires of nodding flowers, and a pleasing color range, from pure white through pinks to some dark maroon-red forms such as *L. martagon* var. *cattaniae.*

The European *L. bulbiferum,* with wide open bowls of orange or rich gold, is the species that has joined with a clutch of lilies from the Far East to produce the hugely successful Asiatic hybrids. It is an exuberant, fast-growing, very early flowering plant, but in cultivation it is best moved and propagated frequently, as it can exhaust a location and die out. Another long-cultivated European, *L. pyrenaicum,* usually the first lily to bloom, is distinctly different. Formerly more widespread in gardens than it is at present, it has bulbs of many narrow scales, lots of narrow, bright green foliage clustered around the stems, and plenty of nodding, dark-spotted Turk's cap flowers, usually colored deep lemon.

AMERICAN AND ASIATIC SPECIES

The settlers in America discovered here a new flora. Lilies were sent back into Europe, but only a few became established garden plants. The most robust proved to be *L. pardalinum,* a useful species that can be planted and left for many years. One of the most prized finds was *L. canadense,* and this remains a favorite of lily fanciers; but, despite its early introduction into Europe by 1629, the secret of growing it well has yet to be discovered. It can flourish in one garden and fail in the one next door, or it can do well for several years and then decline. Its relatively large flowers, in gold or orange, are gracefully held, hanging but with its pointed petals swept in a graceful arc.

The exploration of the East, especially China, was often led by missionaries, many of whom were fascinated by the botanical wildlife of the country and would

L. lancifolium var. splendens is a strong form of an exuberant species that has long been a favorite garden plant and is one of the most important founder species of the Asiatic hybrids.

make collections. Père David was one, and his name is commemorated in the species *L. davidii*, an attractive lily with orange pendent blooms. In gardens it has been somewhat in the shadow of the tiger lily (*L. lancifolium*, formerly *L. tigrinum*), which took to cultivation very easily. This was hardly surprising, as it had been widely grown for centuries as a food plant.

The long-term isolation of Japan from international trade and communication made it difficult to obtain plants indigenous to that country, of which there were several lily species and some hybrids tended by gardeners there. Two kinds were outstanding, distinct from all others and perhaps encapsulating some of the mystery of the East: *L. speciosum* and *L. auratum*. The first has stalked leaves and recurving, nodding flowers in white and pink, all held in airy heads within a cloud of perfume, while the second has large flowers with wide petals and a voluptuous scent. It was flowered in Britain in 1862 and shown at the Royal Horticultural Society in July of that year, where it created a horticultural sensation (see page 14).

Lilium auratum was first shown by the famous Veitch nursery, one of the most active in the nineteenth and twentieth centuries, which arranged for the introduction of many plants from Asia. A major importation of *L. auratum* took place from 1877 to 1879, and it is thought that the numbers being sent to Europe in later years reached into millions. This was not an unqualified success, however, as bulbs were susceptible to basal rot in transit and became prey to virus in European gardens. They fared better in warmer climates, such as Oregon and parts of New Zealand. Nowadays it is the hybrid series from the cross-breeding of *L. auratum* and *L. speciosum* that play a major role in the garden, and these have proved much easier to grow.

China seemed to be an inexhaustible treasure store of all types of lilies, particularly Trumpets, though not all grew with unrestrained vitality in gardens. Most are beautiful white flowers: *L. leucanthum*, *L. longiflorum*, and *L. wallichianum* were plants of the mainland, while *L. philippinense* and *L. formosanum* were named after their island homes. Commercially, *L. longiflorum*, the Easter lily, was by far the most important. It was easy to propagate from seed, and the blooms have for a century been prized as cut flowers; they are grown under glass in Europe and many other countries but will succeed in the open in milder climates. The two yellow-flowered species, *L. sargentiae* and *L. sulphureum*, have proved trickier to keep healthy in gardens but have made a valuable contribution to the breeding of strong golden hybrids. None of these species, however, has had such an impact on the gardening scene in Europe, North America, the Antipodes, and elsewhere as *L. regale*.

THE REGAL LILY STORY

At the turn of the twentieth century, the young Ernest Wilson was engaged by the Veitch nursery to go to China to seek seeds of the handkerchief tree (*Davidia involucrata*) and others. In 1903, he found himself in the Min valley of western Szechwan, a narrow gorge with high, precipitous sides. It happened that a particular lily was in bloom, with thousands of stems leaning from the sides and spilling their perfume on the air. He had discovered the only known habitat of *L. regale*, which some would regard as the most splendid and successful of lilies in our gardens. He described what may have been the most exciting moment in the history of plant hunting:

L. regale is blessed with a robust constitution: the bulbs grow well under cultivation and freely produce seed that develops rapidly into flowering plants.

There, in narrow, semi-arid valleys down which thunder torrents, and encompassed by mountains composed of mudshales and granites, whose peaks are clothed with snow eternal, the Regal Lily has its home. In summer the heat is terrific, in winter the cold is intense, and at all seasons these valleys are subject to sudden and violent windstorms against which neither man nor beast can make headway. There, in June, by the wayside, in rock crevices by the torrent's edge, and high up on the mountainside and precipice, this lily in full bloom greets the weary wayfarer. Not in twos or threes but in hundreds, in thousands, aye, in tens of thousands. Its slender stems, each from two to four feet tall, flexible and tense as steel, overtopping the coarse grass and scrub, are crowned with one to several large funnel-shaped flowers more or less wine-colored without, pure white and lustrous on the face, clear canary-yellow within the tube and each stamen filament tipped with a golden anther. The air in the cool of the morning and in the evening is laden with delicious perfume exhaled from each bloom. For a brief season this lonely, semi-desert is transformed by this Lily into a veritable fairy-land.

Wilson harvested many bulbs and introduced them into the United States and Europe. A consignment of around 3,000 was sent back to Veitch's nursery in the autumn of 1904. It bloomed for the first time in Britain the following year and has been featured in the lists of all the main bulb dealers ever since.

how lilies were first grown

L. auratum caused a sensation when it was introduced into Europe from Japan in the 1860s. With the largest flowers of the genus, perhaps as much as 10–12in. across, it was one of the wonders of the natural world. The wide, open flowers vary in size and in color around a standard white with a star of gold formed by the central stripe down each petal that gave it its common name, gold-banded lily.

Through the nineteenth and early twentieth centuries, new importations of bulbs from the East were eagerly sought. Many of the newly discovered lilies were the playthings of the wealthy and a source of rivalry between the owners of stately homes. The Trumpets were much prized, but probably the most sought after were the *L. auratum* forms. Growers vied with each other to produce the largest flowers and the most massive heads of bloom. In the 1869 September issue of *The Floral World* is a report that is a eulogy to the species and gives a flavor both of the social mores of the time and of the genteel competitive spirit among the aristocracy.

Lilium auratum is only just beginning to show its true capabilities. Messrs. Standish and Co. of Ascot have had a plant in bloom during the past month, with a single stem measuring 13 feet in height, and bearing upwards of a hundred flowers. At a committee meeting of the Royal Horticultural Society, on the 17th ult., Mr Goode, gardener to the Dowager Lady Ashburnam, Melchet Court, Romney, Hants, exhibited a grand specimen, with the main stems nine feet high, measuring 1 inch in diameter at a foot from the surface of the soil, besides smaller stems, bearing altogether 152 flowers—a wonderful example of cultural skill.

Gardeners were inclined almost to force-feed their plants, a regime that usually ended in disaster, as the bulbs were unaccustomed to such rich fare. In its wild home the species was used to the meager diet of the ash soil of quiescent Japanese volcanoes. Cultivators in Europe at the end of the growing season might turn out their pots to find that the bulb had disappeared. There had been no hint of trouble above ground; the stem and flower had been fed and supported by the extensive roots from the stem, an instance of how effective and important this annually renewed stem-rooting can be.

E. H. Wilson writes of seeing the species growing wild:

In Japan there is much poor and hungry soil but none more so than the slopes of august Fiji and the volcanic deposits of the neighboring Idzu province. Around Matsushima, a beauty spot in northern Japan, I saw this Lily in quantity growing in coarse grey sandstone rock. In western Japan, in the province of Uzen, I also met

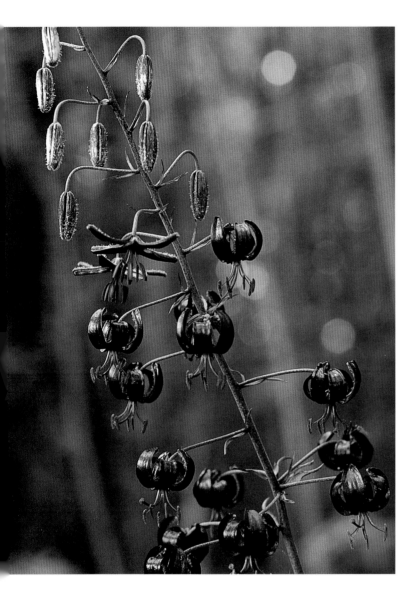

with it growing wild on gravelly banks and hillsides amongst small shrubs and coarse grasses. It is the open, porous soil, and not the rich humus, that this Lily luxuriates in. Leafsoil it loves, in common with all Lilies, but it wants no unaerated acid peat and it loathes raw nitrogenous manures.

I have kept the capital *L* used by Wilson for the word "lily"—I like the idea of our flower being so honored.

Up to the time of the outbreak of the First World War, cottage gardens could boast of clumps of *L. candidum,* often one of the relatively few flowers growing among the vegetables. The species *L. martagon, L. bulbiferum,* and *L. pyrenaicum* might also have been grown, a legacy of the monastery herbal gardens of the Middle Ages. In more sophisticated gardens, much of the effort in lily culture for the 50 or so years before the outbreak of the Second World War was directed toward trying to arrange particular cultural conditions that the imported species would enjoy—an endeavor that tended to be rewarded rather intermittently.

THE ADVANCE OF MODERN HYBRIDS

The Japanese may have been the first to raise large numbers of lilies from seed, using their native species together with kinds introduced from China, of which *L. maculatum* and *L. dauricum* were the most significant. Growing together, they underwent cross-pollination, and a race of hybrid kinds was brought into Europe and

L. martagon var. *cattaniae* 'The Moor' is a selected clone from the dark-flowered form of the species familiar in European gardens for more than five centuries.

marketed by the Dutch growers as *L. × maculatum.* Relatively easy plants to grow, these were the precursors of our modern Asiatic hybrids. During the 1930s and 1940s, the Dutchman Jan de Graaff gathered together as many species and cultivars as he could at his Oregon Bulb Farms and, with a dedicated team, started a huge cross-breeding program (see page 75). Many of the Asiatics could trace some of their ancestry to the *L. × maculatum* series and to the Dutch-raised kinds bred from these with the European species *L. bulbiferum*—hybrid races known as *L. × hollandicum* and *L. × umbellatum.* Some of the resulting seedlings were introduced as Mid-Century Group. And since the middle of the last century most lily types have been successfully hybridized, some more extensively than others, which has given us a huge range of marvelous garden plants.

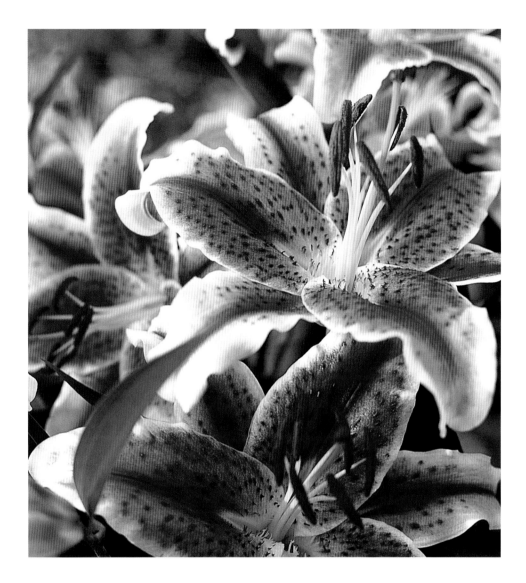

Breeding now takes place in many countries throughout the world. Not only are modern hybrids easy to grow but they can be propagated without any special expertise, which means that commercially huge numbers can be grown rapidly. The cut-flower industry uses millions of bulbs, where gardens are using thousands or tens of thousands; therefore, much more work is done to produce cultivars that make good cut flowers. Upward-facing kinds are the easiest to cut and pack, so these dominate the market. Since the 1950s, the Asiatics have been the backbone of the flower trade, but now the larger cultivars derived from hybridizing the Easter lily (*L. longiflorum*) with the Asiatics, commonly called LA hybrids, are taking over the florists, as they grow easily and have larger flowers. They also have in their favor the ease with which flowers can be produced at any time of the year.

The Dutch flower market at Aalsmeer handles huge quantities of lilies that are exported all over the

'Stargazer' has proved the most successful of the florist lilies in the United States and Britain, where it is probably the most important cut flower of any kind ever cultivated.

world, so that they have become a familiar part of every florist's display. In the year 2000, the prize for the greatest acreage of an individual cultivar was easily won by 'Stargazer' with 556 acres, while the white Oriental 'Siberia' came second with 459 acres. The gardener also benefits from this intensive breeding. The LA hybrids are marvelous garden plants, and the straightforward Asiatics are still available in a wide variety. Dwarf kinds, particularly suitable for pot culture, have established a strong niche in the market. The fantastic Oriental hybrids make choice cut flowers, so they are being intensively bred, and gardeners with neutral or acidic soil can make exotic pictures with these lilies in the open, while others use them as effectively as pot plants. And now we have a series of hybrids from the blending of Orientals with the bloodline of *L. henryi*, giving a wonderful set of plants that inherit the alkaline-tolerant character of the species.

what is a lily?

The name "lily" has been used loosely for many hundreds of years, often to mean little more than "flower"—possibly one with some resemblance to a true lily. A glance at the list of "false" lilies (see page 155) will show that there are many of these, and all but one are not even members of the large lily family, let alone of the *Lilium* genus. Perhaps we should give some specifications for a real lily.

The genus belongs to the Northern Hemisphere, with 80–100 species scattered through Europe, Asia, and North America. They are all bulbous plants, though the form of the bulb varies considerably, and plant size ranges from a few inches high to over 10 feet tall. Plants generally die down for the winter, with only *L. candidum* and one or two rare species maintaining a rosette of leaves through the winter to gain evergreen status.

The lily is a dynamo of energy, in a hurry to grow, bloom, and increase. The seeds are flat disks that are piled up like plates in the seed pod—two piles in each of the three chambers—and it is not unusual to harvest over a hundred viable seeds from a pod. In the wild, as the ripe pod splits this seed will fall and be blown around to suitable and unsuitable nursery spots. Usually only a tiny proportion will germinate to grow to flowering-sized plants. Under controlled conditions, however, the gardener can often achieve an almost 100-percent germination rate.

The seedlings of most lilies produce a single cotyledon leaf, strap-shaped and often carrying the seed case like a flag at its tip. Shortly after the first true leaf appears, elliptic or spear-shaped, tiny bulbs start to be formed. Some lily types skip the cotyledon stage by forming embryo bulbs with roots by the side of the seed, breaking through the soil surface with their first true leaves not until much later. Given suitable conditions, the small bulbs of most types grow quickly, doubling, quadrupling, and further increasing their bulk in a matter of a few weeks. This process is accompanied by the production of more leaves until there is a mini-rosette of foliage. Stronger plants may try to produce a wiry stem with a complement of little leaves in the first growing season, but most will wait for their second year to do this and may or may not manage to top their stem with a bloom.

LILY BULBS

All the most popular lilies, such as the Asiatic hybrids, the Trumpets, and the Orientals, have round, concentric bulbs made up of scales that are concave and wrap around the inner scales and growing center. The scales can be narrow and tightly incurved, but are more usually wide enough to encircle a quarter, a third, or even half of the bulb. The flowering stem arises through

Lilies are normally very generous with their seed, and *L. martagon*, shown here, could be the most profligate of all. Since each pod may contain 40–100 seeds, one can gauge the proportions of a possible population explosion.

the middle, often called a "nose." After the growing season the stem dies down and, in doing so, will often divide the bulb into two. The two new growing points are clearly seen; depending on the age and vigor of the bulbs, the tissue joining the two potential new bulbs will begin to fail and twins result.

Some American species, including *L. pardalinum*, and their hybrids have a different lifestyle. The bulbs have scales, but these are openly scattered along a rhizomatous rootstock, with only the growing points having newer, paler scales gathered together to show where the next flowering stems will emerge. The older scales and rootstock persist for a considerable time, so that over the years an undisturbed bulb will form a wide mat of rootstock and scales. Gardeners impatient to propagate such bulbs will be forced to operate with a sharp knife, making sure that each severed portion has at least one growing point (see page 142). One or two species, such as *L. canadense*, appear to have ordinary concentric bulbs, but by the end of the season each of these may have sent sideways one or more thick stolons, like reaching arms, at the end of which new bulbs form.

A few Asian species, such as *L. duchartrei*, employ yet another method of bulb increase; they are known as stoloniferous-stemmed bulbs. The bulbs send up stems from what look like traditional concentric bulbs, but instead of heading straight for the surface they wander around below, and at intervals along this wayward stem new bulbs form. The stem eventually breaks the surface and does the traditional lily performance. The gardener needs to be careful working around these plants, as there is no telling where the underground stem and new bulbs might be. Sometimes the flowering stem can be as far away as 1–2 feet from its parent bulb. Unrelated lilies, both species and hybrids, may on occasion make a weak attempt to copy this behavior. Certainly it is never wise to assume that a bulb is directly below the flowering stem—a warning that is best heeded when inserting canes or other supports after bulbs have been planted.

THE ROOTS

Roots emerge from the basal "plate" of the bulb, to which the scales are affixed. These roots are of two types. There are fat, strong ones, clearly marked with a series of rings, and these plunge deep in the ground and are able to contract, accordian-wise, to pull bulbs lower down into the soil. This is a valuable operation, particularly with stem bulbils that fall to the ground and need to make their way deeper down to establish themselves. The more numerous roots are the fibrous ones, which with their multitude of root hairs make intimate contact with the soil and feed the plant from the nutrient-laden soil water.

Many lilies also develop roots from the stem between the bulb and the soil surface. In some these roots are a token feature, but in most they form an extensive

1 Concentric bulbs Most lily bulbs are concentric; they vary in size and depth but are basically formed of concave scales, tightly arranged around the central growing point. Some narrow scales are looser.

2 Concentric bulbs with waisted scales Bulbs of the *L. martagon* group have waisted scales that are easily fractured at this narrower point.

3 Rhizomatous bulbs A number of American species have these unusual bulbs. The scales are so brittle that if they are roughly handled, a shower of scales falls away. Each scale has the potential to become a new plant but a badly depleted bulb will be somewhat weakened until it gets reestablished.

4 Stoloniferous bulbs These bulbs of *L. canadense* show how a parent bulb sends out strong stolons to the side, with new bulbs forming at the end of each. This method of bulbous increase is used by only a few species, but where one of these feels happy the method will quickly establish a good stand.

network that undertakes two jobs—the effective augmentation of the feeding system and an anchor for the stem. The stem bearing flowers could easily be rocked to and fro without the support offered by the rooted part of the stem. These stem roots are not usually equally distributed along the stem but appear as so many rings, with lesser numbers between.

LILY FOLIAGE

Lily leaves are normally elliptic, but they vary in width, color, and method of display. It is supposed that the evolutionary prototype lily had leaves arranged in whorls, as in those of the present-day *L. martagon* and *L. pardalinum*. However, the more usual fashion is to have leaves scattered up the stem, sometimes with an incipient spiral pattern discernible. Some lilies have a wealth of leaves; others are sparingly endowed. They may be clasped tightly to the stem, but examples can be found at every intermediate stage up to those held at right angles to the stem or even arching downward. Normally they are joined directly to the stem, but some

SOME FORMS OF LILY FOLIAGE

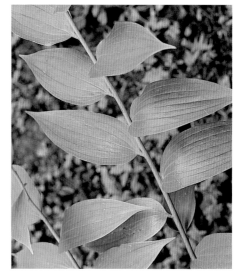

Whorled foliage Members of the Martagon Group and a considerable number of North American species have their foliage arranged in formal whorls. The lower whorls are larger than those above, and toward the top of the stem there may be individual leaflets.

Scattered foliage This is the most usual form of lily foliage. Trumpet lilies often have tall stems with lots of very narrow leaves, sometimes darkly colored, while Asiatic hybrids usually have fleshier, broader leaves that are bright green, though in some the foliage may be suffused with some darker coloring.

Lilium speciosum **foliage** Several of the Oriental species have some or all of their leaves held by distinct leaf stems. The leaves are often arranged alternately up the stem and are more spear-shaped than many. They can give a "classier" feel to the assemblage.

L. lancifolium var. flaviforum,
showing dark bulbils in the leaf
axils, a characteristic of all forms
of the species.

Eastern species, the Orientals, and their hybrid derivatives may have leaf stalks that give a distinct appearance and a more airy manner. Leaf color ranges from pale green to a darkened purple that can be almost black.

LILY STEMS

The speed with which lilies grow in the spring is exciting. Once they have broken through the surface, one can almost stand and watch them rocket upward. The stems of most are as strong and erect as bamboos; indeed, the dead stems can often be used as temporary canes. Many species grow wild in scrubland, and here the arching stems of a few kinds may lean on their neighbors for extra support. Stem color may be an unblemished green, but this is often suffused with a dark purple-maroon that can be so intense as to make them appear black, as in *L. lancifolium* or 'Festival'. Dark stems may or may not be matched to deep-toned foliage and dark flowers.

The obvious job of the stems is to support foliage and flowers, and this may not be a light task, since a payload of 50–100 sizeable flowers is possible. The stems may have another function. Many lily types will produce bulblets on the length of stem below ground, these varying from tiny embryo ones to others as large as marbles or golf balls. A lesser number of lilies will mimic the behavior of the tiger lily (*L. lancifolium*) by manufacturing large quantities of dark bulbils in the leaf axils. Sometimes more than one is grown in the leaf axil, and, since there are plenty of leaves, a stem may give birth to a hundred or so bulbils. There is competition to be the "mother of the year."

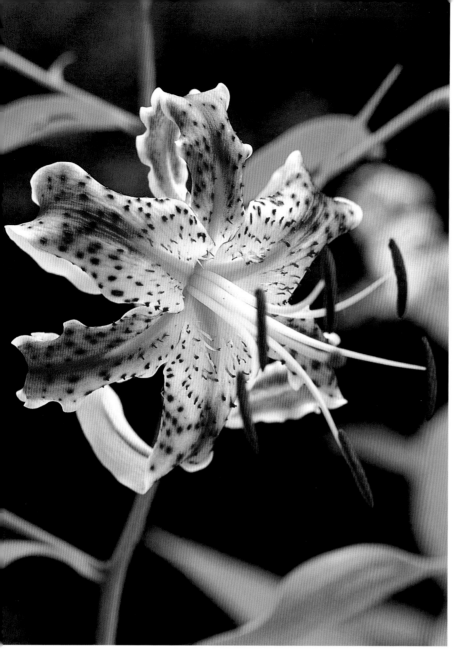

The late-flowering *L. speciosum* is outward- or downward-facing and is one of the most elegant of all lilies.

LILY FLOWERS

We move from the working parts to the main glory of the plant. Few can fail to be impressed by the floral displays of a lily, which can range from one or two flowers only a few inches high (as in *L. formosanum* var. *pricei* or some of the species from Tibet) to the towering heads of dozens of flowers held up to 10 feet aloft. The number of blooms can border on the ridiculously prolific; I remember as a six-year-old helping my father count a total of more than 150 flowers on a stem of *L. davidii* var. *willmottiae*. A similar count is possible on a well-grown, well-established bulb of 'Black Beauty'.

The color palette is wide, from white (sometimes greenish) to deepest yellow, and from orange to red. A new Antipodean lily is described as "black." The permutations of color combination are numerous, sometimes one color merging with or overlying another. Contrasting shades or colors can be applied as beauty spots, veining, picotee work (pale, edged with a darker color), or laid on as brushstrokes.

The pose of flowers is important, and here the cut-flower market has exerted a huge influence on breeding. The need for easily cut and packed flowers has meant that upward-facing cultivars exceed outward-facing and pendent kinds by a ratio far in excess of a hundred to one. This turns on its head the usual dress mode of wild lilies, which favor a pendent or semi-pendent pose, the better to protect their pollen supplies and the receptive stigmas. There are nevertheless important species, such as *L. bulbiferum* and *L. dauricum*, that rebel and blatantly display sky-staring flowers seeking to attract passing insects to help with pollination.

While the gardener sees the flower as one having six petals, the botanist sees an outer ring of three sepals and an inner ring of three petals; if he deigns to amalgamate them, he maintains his professional dignity by terming them "tepals." We shall be happy with "petals." These may be more or less even-textured, but will have nectary channels leading toward the center for the convenience of insects. The nectary channels may be differently colored, perhaps green, to paint a central six-pointed star. Some kinds have a number of raised pimples on the inner surfaces, eruptions that are more correctly termed papillae. *L. henryi* curls back

The pendent *L. henryi* makes a feature of its papillae, a pattern of eruptions that are completely natural and call for no medical diagnosis. Other species have similar features, though usually less numerous, but sometimes made conspicuous by being flecked with an alternative petal colour.

its petals to display numerous large papillae, and *L. speciosum* and Oriental hybrids are usually fairly well endowed, the papillae often being made more noticeable by having their tips touched with color.

While the normal complement is six petals, there are cultivars in which the sexual parts—stamens and stigma— have been transmuted into petaloids to give double flowers. In some, such as the Asiatic 'Fata Morgana', the extra petals are somewhat smaller and more or less overlie the original six; the doubling is certainly not excessive and could be overlooked at a distance. 'Pamela Jean' is a lightly doubled orange LA hybrid and there is a series marketed as Kiss Lilies that are dwarf Asiatics without pollen, most of which have the traditional six petals but some tend to produce a number of extra smaller petals.

There are now a number of more formidable doubles, flowers that look clearly distinct from traditional types. An Australian lily, 'Miss Lucy', is a starry white flower with just a whisper of green and pink that has up to 18 petals, the extra ones initially gathered together to form a projecting nose from the center of each bloom. An American lily bred by the specialist Judith Freeman outdoes all other doubles. It is an Oriental called 'Flying Circus', with up to 50 petals! There are so many that the flower reaches forward, with six or seven layers of pointed petals. Opening in shades of pale green, the blooms end up pure white as the flower opens, reaches out, and matures over a period of weeks through mid- to late summer. It will certainly shock the purist.

'Snow Star' clearly displays the upward-facing pose of the vast majority of Asiatic hybrids.

The form of the flower can be described as trumpet, bowl-shaped, starry, or recurving, or as "Turk's cap." This last is really an outdated reference to the suggested similarity in appearance to the Turkish headwear abolished early in the twentieth century and now usually met with only in theatrical Turkish characters. The usefulness of the term will probably ensure its survival to describe the rolled-back form of flowers such as those of *L. martagon* or *L. lancifolium*.

We now move into the garden and are ready to deploy our bulbs. Lilies can lay claim to being the ideal plants for the twenty-first-century garden, as they grow rapidly, they enjoy the company of shrubs and other plants, and they die down quite discreetly. Potted bulbs on the point of bloom can be brought forward to enliven the patio or any other part of the garden and can be dropped into a border,

introducing lilies: in the garden

In this skillfully assembled midsummer medley, pink outward-facing lilies form the undoubted centerpiece without detracting from the appeal of their flowering companions—the deep magenta-colored *Geranium* 'Ann Folkard' and purple-blue annual *Cerinthe major*.

either sitting on the ground or sunk in it. With gardens generally getting smaller, portable pots of lilies are a godsend, being easy to grow and so effective.

Lilies are one of the most glamorous "stars" of our beds and borders, viewed as we move around the garden or seen from the house, and a group of lilies brings the garden to life. While there may be places in the garden where bulbs of new cultivars can be tried out and assessed, they may not be expected to play a major part in the overall garden design. But in the garden proper we can plan with some forethought, and here boldness can often be our watchword. Lilies are not self-effacing—even a very few bulbs will make a major impact on the garden scene. Soil, light, and shelter will all influence the end result in the first season, and this can extend into the displays of future years. It is one of the pleasing features of horticulture that there are no absolutes of design or technique. However, a few suggestions may save us from some pitfalls, and our plant celebrities will definitely benefit from careful handling.

There is certainly no harm in planting single bulbs of cultivars, and they can be exciting growing among other plants. But we are likely to derive greater benefit from a few bold plantings than from the scattered contribution of singletons. This does not mean that we need deprive ourselves of a wide selection of lilies, because by choosing cultivars that bloom at different periods, we can afford relatively close plantings without conflicts of color or habit that are likely to irritate us.

We encounter a mathematical enigma here. If we plant a group of three lilies, few would doubt that the resulting effect is far more than three times that of the singleton. A group of five or more will be even more beguiling. By the same token, the planting of mixed cultivars is likely to be less successful than separate groups of different kinds. Each cultivar has its own character, height, and flowering period; plants from mixed bags of bulbs could well be of varying heights and flowering periods, reducing the overall effect.

stars of the border

There are types of lily for all situations; the colors and forms are various, and most are inexpensive plants. While some writers may be dogmatic about color planning in the garden, such exposition is often of limited value since some people simply enjoy certain colors more than others. In general, yellows, oranges, and reds tend to be rather more extrovert in the garden than whites, creams, and pinks. Nature seems to ensure that most colors can live together, and there are certain combinations that seem complementary. For example, the vibrant maroons, purples, and magentas of geranium species can highlight neighboring lilies that are white, cream, or yellow. And the drama of orange and red lilies will be even further highlighted by the soft greens of ferns, grasses, and other plants. But to start listing lily cultivars and other flowering plants as boon companions is a little like backing horses—luck enters into the equation. The same cultivar may bloom at a slightly different time each year and miss its planned cue.

A SUCCESSION OF BLOOM

Some thought toward providing a succession of lily blooms, on the other hand, really does pay dividends. There are earlyflowering species and some Asiatic cultivars that bloom at the end of spring. Others, especially the Asiatics, will be handed the baton to see summer well into its reign. Then the Trumpets begin their fanfare toward midsummer, before most of the Orientals in the open garden amaze us with their flowers. Later-flowering Orientals then take us into fall.

Bulbs raised in pots can bring earlier flowers with some manipulation of their environments, and with a little more care, the performance of others can be retarded. Delaying bloom is certainly trickier than forcing bulbs into earlier flower. As a rule of thumb, one can assume that potted bulbs will come into bloom 100 days, or approximately 14 weeks, after planting. This applies to culture in a protected, frost-free environment but without undue heat. To delay flowering, the most practical method is simply to plant later. Bulbs can be kept in limbo by being stored in cool conditions such as the domestic refrigerator—but not in the freezer compartment. Make sure that the stored bulbs are free of disease, plump, and a reasonable size before placing them in store. Avoid bulbs showing any signs of growth, such as shoots emerging from the bulb. It would be wise to dip them in systemic fungicide prior to storing and allow them to become more or less dry before their "hibernation." With an occasional check, it should be possible to keep the bulbs in store for several weeks or even months before planting.

Without any manipulation, in the garden the earliest lilies into bloom will include *L. pyrenaicum* and *L. bulbiferum*, followed by such cultivars as 'Red Carpet', 'Fire King', and 'Harmony'. Many Asiatics will quickly follow, and then Trumpets such as *L. regale*, Golden Splendor Group, and Pink Perfection Group start a prolonged display. Few gardens with any pretensions to an interest in lilies will be without the highly scented *L. regale*, perhaps the favorite of the species with gardeners in temperate regions. Asiatics overlap the flowering period of the Trumpets, and some of the standard kinds will be augmented by more unusual ones, such as the semi-double 'Fata Morgana', which can be in bloom for a prolonged period. Later Asiatics will include 'Grand Cru' and one of the latest-flowering of all, Yellow Blaze Group. The Orientals cover a long period with some, like 'Mona Lisa', opening relatively early, while those closer to *L. speciosum*, such as 'Journey's End', are likely to bloom later.

Orange Asiatic lilies (above) join the extrovert, hot-colored display of dahlias and chrysanthemums, offset by the sword-like foliage of irises and crocosmias.

There is a large number of golden Asiatics (opposite) that grow very easily and are good mixers, their yellow color echoed here by tall foxtail lilies (*Eremurus*).

SOILS AND SITES

Soils are important. The most important feature of lily-friendly soils is drainage, or more specifically a soil structure that is open with plenty of air in it and thus well drained. Most lily types revel in soil rich in humus; leaf mold and well made composts are much appreciated, though unrotted farmyard manure will not be welcome. Humus-rich conditions are likely to result in soils that are either neutral or slightly acidic, which is exactly what the majority of lilies like. Most Asiatics and Trumpets are tolerant of some alkalinity, especially if there is humus in the soil. The one group that finds alkaline soil impossible is the Orientals, the progeny of *L. speciosum* and *L. auratum*, and to them alkalinity is fatal. The Japanese *L. speciosum* can be lovely in neutral soils or ones on the acidic side of the pH spectrum but impossible in very alkaline soil. Preparing soil for lilies is usually a matter of thorough digging and incorporating generous quantities of well-rotted organic matter. Do not be deterred if growing lilies in heavy clays or other soils that might seem unpromising (for more information on soils, see pages 130–32).

In borders it is usual to plant taller lilies toward the back of a border, or in the middle of island beds, with the dwarf kinds placed near the front. This is not an absolute rule, and there may be sites where you want to have an impressive stand of *L. regale* or another of the Trumpets much closer to the front, to emphasize their height and provide a formidable punctuation point.

While it is now more usual to deploy lilies in an integrated garden scheme, in the past some fanciers provided their bulbs with a special lily bed. This is still done by some growers. It has the advantage of allowing you to organize the site to meet the plants' requirements as exactly as possible. One feature of such beds is that the sides are often built up so that the soil level is higher than the surrounding ground, making the all-important drainage easier to manage. The soil can be enriched with well-rotted compost, and grit can be added to make the whole bed an approximation of the mix one might arrange in a pot or other container. It may also be rather easier to monitor the health of plants and deal with diseases and pests in these privileged surroundings.

Examples of Pink Perfection Group (above) are impressive in size, color, and form and create a highly scented display in any garden.

In a romantic association (opposite), the fragrant *L. regale* is seen with herbaceous perennials *Stachys byzantina* and delphiniums.

ASSOCIATION WITH OTHER PLANTS

Lilies are good mixers. They enjoy company. Their gregarious nature is displayed both in the rather theatrical environment of potted plants on the patio and when growing in garden borders or naturalized in wilder areas. This is not to say that they are jungle plants; what they enjoy is to have some shade from other plants around their roots but to have much of their foliage as well as their flower heads

In the lee of the shrub *Hydrangea arborescens* 'Annabel', scented white *L. regale* open their trumpet blooms alongside the thistle-like *Eryngium giganteum*, feverfew (*Tanacetum parthenium*), and the shapely heads of dying alliums.

rejoicing in the air and sunshine. No snobbery is effected—they will be perfectly happy with annuals such as love-in-a-mist (*Nigella*), cornflower (*Centaurea cyanus*), larkspur (*Consolida ambigua*), or candytuft (*Iberis umbellata*). When bulbs are planted in the fall or early spring, seed of annuals can be scattered over the site to provide company and extra flowers, and these simple annuals will be happy to act as auxiliaries—the chorus line behind the star. There may be another benefit of this procedure. The bare patch of ground where bulbs have been planted will be given into the caretaking of these annuals, which will remind us that there are bulbs in place and will preclude any disastrous incursion into the soil to plant other items.

PERENNIALS

More permanent neighbors could include some of the hardy geranium species and their hybrids. The flower colors are often complementary, but the contrasting foliage is as important. In this respect hostas can provide a fine ground cover of differing foliage, while they also cast shade around the lilies' toes. Hostas will need to be housed to the side of the bulbs, as few plants can grow in direct competition with their extrovert rooting system. Achilleas and some of the tamed thistles, such as the biennial *Eryngium giganteum*, might be useful growing with groups of lilies. If this plant begins to be a little too invasive, the number of seedlings allowed to see a second year can be reduced.

GRASSES AND FERNS

The popularity of grasses remains high. Many of the middle-sized and smaller kinds can form interesting communities with lilies, and they will always be complementary plants, unlikely to clash with the star's performance. Suitable grasses may be large, like the 8-foot-tall giant feather grass (*Stipa gigantea*), with its elegant flowering heads of sparkling silvery spikelets. Smaller grasses could include sedges such as *Carex oshimensis* 'Evergold', with its tussocks of yellow-striped arching leaves, the plants being only some 8 inches high. Intermediate in size will be some of the graceful *Miscanthus sinensis* forms, with very slender leaves. The pendulous sedge (*Carex pendula*) can be effective and in bloom at the same time as the lilies, with long flowers hanging like catkins from rodlike angled stems.

Hardy ferns offer another well-tried combination. There are deciduous and evergreen kinds in various sizes, and many of these can be grown in open sites—

Brilliant vermilion Asiatics such as 'Gran Paradiso' and its seedling 'Castello' make a striking splash of colour whatever their neighbours.

they are not all shade lovers. Some forms of the scaly male fern and the male fern (*Dryopteris affinis* and *D. filix-mas*) are very hardy in open sites and make decorative 2-foot-high plants, the 'Grandiceps' series being decorated with tasseled crests. The lady fern (*Athyrium filix-femina*) is as hardy and very graceful; there are a number of smaller forms. Indeed, the number of good ferns is legion.

SHRUBS

Shrubs are natural lily allies. In the wild, they are often closely associated, many lilies finding the shrubs a help in terms of support and protection from weather and animal predations. In the garden they are also useful, perhaps giving some frost protection early on and always lending each other distinction. The only possible snag is that some shrubs grow surprisingly fast, quickly enough to sometimes smother lilies. But this should not prove too great a problem—threatened bulbs can simply be moved at the end of the growing season.

The root systems of shrubs help to structure the soil and will aid drainage. Soil water will be allowed to drain downward and the shrubs will be taking up a lot of moisture, helping to even out the moisture content of the soil mass. On the whole, this will be helpful to the bulbs, which enjoy a ready supply of water through their growing period but are chary of excesses through the more dormant months of winter.

Rhododendrons and lilies are a well-established partnership, the shrubs enjoying an alkaline soil and this being very acceptable to the bulbs also. Camellias can join the party. These shrubs will be far enough away not to inconvenience the bulbs' extrovert rooting system, and they will have finished their flowering well before the lilies perform. The dark evergreen foliage of both these shrubs adds gravitas to the ensemble. The medium-size spiraeas, *Brachyglottis* (*Senecio*), and forms of *Viburnum* are other obvious friendly companions. It is difficult to think of any shrubs, either evergreen or deciduous, that do not go well with our lilies.

'Royal Gold' is a strong-growing, mid-season flowering lily, often called 'the golden regal'. It grows well with other plants and makes a long-lasting clump that blooms freely and floods the garden with perfume.

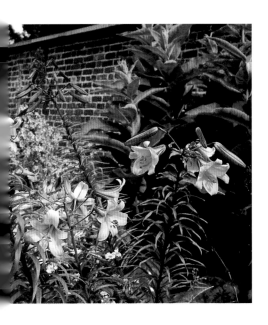

There are few plants to avoid altogether, but I would certainly be careful in siting daylilies (*Hemerocallis*) too close. The flowers are lily-shaped and often in similar enough colors to cause some slight visual confusion. It is far better to have contrasting floral and foliar effects. Nor would one want fast-encroaching neighbors, such as vigorous asters, that could overwhelm the more measured growth of the lilies.

lilies for pots and containers

We want our lilies to be happy, but we also want to have them on view. Pots or other containers, being mobile, allow many lilies to be brought into close proximity to the house or certainly in view from it. As one group of lilies passes out of bloom, it can be moved away and replaced by another in bud. Such pots can join other types of container-grown plants to make a pleasing grouping, turning the patio into a fully furnished outdoor room.

Lilies grow easily in containers and are far more drought-resistant than most plants, so they are very amenable. While they may manage very well with little moisture, they do, of course, need life-giving water. Plant growth will have been massive since the bulbs were first planted and watering the newly emerging shoots was easy, but it becomes progressively more difficult to water as the plants grow. Stems and leaves crowd the pots, and the plants are taking up increasing quantities of water at a time of year when warmer weather is hastening transpiration through the leaves. It becomes almost impossible to water from above or to gauge how far the water has penetrated downward. It is far better to have some means close by to stand the pots in water and allow them to draw up enough until the soil is thoroughly saturated.

The versatility of pot plants is demonstrated by several benefits. The soil or mixture in which bulbs are growing is under the gardener's complete control (see pages 134–37), and containers are mobile, so they can be moved around the garden. The plants will be easy to monitor for general health and specific diseases and pests—slugs are likely to find the pots a complete no-go area. Then, at the end of the growing cycle, bulbs can be turned out, shaken free of soil, inspected, divided, and replanted, either again in pots or out in the open—or half and half. Repotted bulbs can be overwintered easily.

Every year there seems to be a wider variety of lilies especially suited to pot culture. The vast majority of hybrids, even the taller kinds, grow easily in containers, and many of the species make excellent container subjects. Those that would serve with distinction could include *L. amabile, L. auratum, L. bulbiferum, L. cernuum, L. longiflorum, L. pumilum, L. regale,* and *L. speciosum.* Some species are less ready to grow easily in the confinement of pots, however, and these include some of the rhizomatous North American species and those with rather more staid habits of growth, such as *L. martagon, L. hansonii,* and *L. pardalinum.* However, even these can be managed in large containers.

The importance of the lily as a pot plant is clearly reflected in the work of breeders, who since the 1980s have been bringing out new

The repetition of container-grown regal lilies gives the planting a sense of formality, while their scent will enchant those who ascend or descend the steps.

In an informal container grouping, trailing blue lobelia and pelargoniums happily partner *L*. 'Arena' to bring a patio to life.

cultivars and series that are sturdy dwarfs. The value of dwarf Asiatics and dwarf Orientals as pot or patio plants was instantly recognized, and many bulbs now sold to gardeners are these short-stemmed kinds, welladapted to container culture as well as being useful toward the front of a garden bed. They are usually only 10–20 inches high, though they can be shorter. 'Denia' is an early blush-pink lily that reaches only about 8 inches. This and the other dwarfs have relatively large flowers, making a colorful contribution but perhaps lacking in some of the grace that is the birthright of so many other lilies. The range of colors among dwarf lilies is now extensive; the flowers are often pointed stars, but others are more bowl-shaped. As they are low-growing, the selected seedlings tend to be those with upward-facing flowers, with a few having blooms bent slightly sideways.

The Pixie series of Asiatics is well established and recognized as easy, sturdy plants that will never need support and can manage in exposed conditions. They tend to bloom early and will come several weeks earlier still if planted in good time and grown under glass. The color range covers most lily shades from white and yellow to orange, red, and crimson, and their heights vary between 12 and 18 inches.

There are other dwarf kinds marketed either as a series or as individuals. Short-stemmed Orientals include 'Garden Party', with white flowers with tiny pink dots, each petal having a central golden stripe ending rosy red to emphasize the star form; it stands some 2 feet tall. Others such as 'Mr. Ed', 'Mr. Ruud', and 'Mr. Sam' are shorter at 12–16 inches. 'Mona Lisa' grows to some 20 inches and is a favorite, with typical Oriental flowers, broad petals edged white but warmly colored in shades of pink. These all have the added attraction of a pleasing perfume.

It would be wrong to suggest that only the dwarf types should be used in pots, and it will certainly help to achieve variety to have lilies of different habits and postures to bring to the fore. The Trumpets, such as *L. regale*, and the hybrids Pink Perfection Group, African Queen Group, and 'Royal Gold' ought to be given their chance on stage. Later, some end-of-season types such as *L. speciosum* and hybrids such as 'Journey's End' will be invaluable at a time when one may be tiring of the traditional summer flowers, which are just beginning to fail and suggest the imminent need to tidy up for the winter season. Take an intoxicating breath of the lilies' perfume, and forget about the work to come.

The larger the container, the easier it is to grow lilies successfully (see pages 134–35); almost anything that can contain soil will serve, provided we remember the mantra "lilies like drainage." Generous containers, such as half-tubs, can be home to such species as *L. regale*, which will delight by sight and perfume for weeks but can also cohabit with other plants that will take on decorative duties before and after the lilies' display. They can proceed to an afterlife in the border, or, if they are looked after, the bulbs can be shaken out before the winter and repotted, perhaps removing smaller offspring to be grown on for a season in a nursery spot.

Having safely planted bulbs in a large container, one is left with what looks like empty potting mix crying out for plants. We have the choice of adding some other forms of plant life through which the lilies will grow or allowing the pot to be devoted to the culture of lilies alone. Larger pots, tubs, or other receptacles may look better with extra plants, even if these are of modest demeanor. Trailing lobelia or other small bedding annuals can cover the soil and take away some of the pot's starkness, while providing interest and beauty before and after the drama of the lily flowers. They can also help to shade the soil, cover the bulbs, and maintain a more equable temperature. Marguerites, grasses, ivies, and all the flowering plants associated with hanging baskets can be called on for this auxiliary service. Scented-leaved pelargoniums' much-divided leaves can be effective in their own right and make a real contrast to the lilies.

Someone new to lilies will almost always try them first in pots, but after flowering the entire potful of lilies may be introduced into the garden border. Potted lilies can be extremely useful in the wider garden context, especially when

The vivid dwarf lily 'Orange Pixie' is grouped with pots of different heights containing foliage plants such as hostas, grasses and lady's mantle (*Alchemilla mollis*).

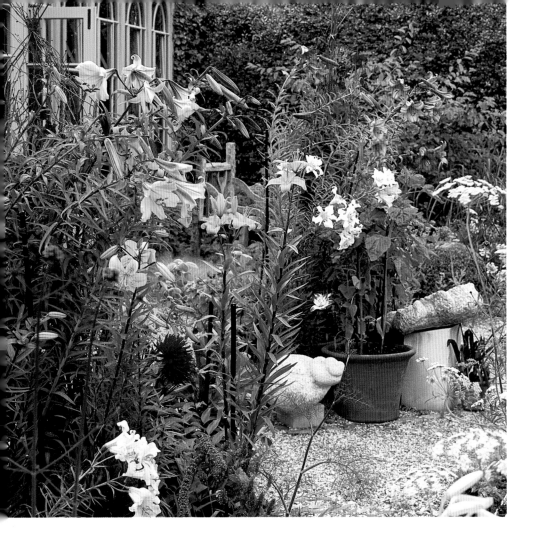

herbaceous plants are past their best. They need not be restricted to the greenhouse, sunroom, or patio but can be introduced between shrubs or elsewhere in borders to enliven the scene. The pot can either be placed on the ground or sunk into the soil to look more natural. Oriental poppies, for example, are splendid in bloom but when cut away after flowering may leave a considerable gap—a pot of lilies will fill the vacuum. They may also add color to areas that are all foliage until late in the year. Japanese anemones (*Anemone* × *hybrida*) are usually late into flower, and you may be able to squeeze a pot of lilies in among them to brighten the picture. This lesson has been learned in many

Lilies predominate in a large container grouping near the house. Prominent among them are the tall, colorful Pink Perfection Group and yellow Golden Splendor Group.

public gardens. On Monday the garden may appear all right, but on Tuesday it is transformed with the excitement of lilies just coming into bloom. They look completely natural and as if they have been developing in their stations since the spring. Much of gardening is about cheating—or, rather, stage management and manipulation.

"WAITING ROOMS"

Space in our smaller gardens is always at a premium, and we want to make the most of what we have. The patio and areas close to the house are for our own enjoyment, often an important adjunct to the living area of the house, where we can take our ease or enjoy a cup of coffee or a glass of wine. At their peak, our lilies, in brilliant colors and forms, may also intoxicate with perfume. But to have a series of pots to bring into prominent spots through the growing months, we need somewhere to keep the developing potfuls waiting in the wings.

Our waiting area need not be elaborate—a square yard or two near the greenhouse may serve, or perhaps just a space behind some shrubs. Sometimes the greenhouse is housed in a site that has a passageway at the blind side, and this may well become our plant "waiting room." Most gardens are likely to have one or more small areas away from the main focus of attention, where a few containers will not look amiss.

lilies as wild plants

L. martagon grows with grasses in a completely naturalistic setting. It has grown and increased for many decades in this large country garden where it now numbers into many thousands.

A large number of lilies can be planted and more or less left to manage for themselves for decades. If the right spots are chosen, they will be happy to pay the rent of their space with an annual display and will probably increase steadily in numbers. To gain the most appealing effect from naturalized lilies, the closer we can approach an apparently natural appearance, the more successful we shall be. The aim is to have them growing as if they had arrived of their own accord and settled in permanently. Using a single cultivar, an initial group of three to perhaps a dozen bulbs can be planted; then, at a distance of a few yards, a smaller group can be introduced. Rounded or elliptical clusters will look right; lines will not. They can appear to be taking advantage of spaces between shrubs or trees as they might in the wild. Some will grow in unmown grass, perhaps accompanied by other long-lived perennials such as peonies.

Some hybrids, such as those of the Martagons, are fertile and produce plenty of seed, which can be collected and sown either in the open or in containers. Small bulbs can be planted out after a couple of seasons, though they may take a few more years to reach full flowering size. The species *L. monadelphum, L. martagon,* and *L. pyrenaicum* can be successful self-seeders. *L. henryi* and *L. candidum* may set seed, but are less likely to do so or to produce natural seedlings in most gardens.

What suits one kind of lily may not be what another wants, so it is worth looking individually at lily species suitable for naturalizing. *L. candidum* needs an airy, sunny spot where the sun can reach the soil and where it will not be overshadowed by its neighbors. It has several unusual characteristics: it seems to enjoy warmth around its bulb, it certainly likes very good drainage, and it is alone in being best planted with the bulbs barely covered with soil. Plant these bulbs when they are available; if there is a choice, the best time will be when the flowering stem is beginning to wither. If you can obtain freshly dug bulbs—perhaps from a friend's garden—these are likely to do much better than those that have been some weeks in a plastic bag in a garden center. However, these packaged bulbs will settle down in time, and if they do not do brilliantly the first season, do not lose heart, as they will probably begin to shine the following year. Once planted, either as a single bulb or as a group of three or more, they will normally behave best if left alone—five or ten years without moving is possible.

While we know that *L. martagon* can flourish in a garden for many years, it may not be the easiest kind to make an immediate effect. Freshly lifted bulbs will root and grow well in a wide variety of soils, including slightly alkaline ones. Bulbs that have been stored for a time after lifting may sulk; when planted, they can root but may balk at producing a stem above ground. But after a season all is well, and they flower and grow normally. Bulbs split steadily rather than dramatically; any brittle scales that break away will soon form small bulbs, but these will take several

L. pyrenaicum has a name to indicate its home but it does well in temperate gardens in various parts of the world. There have been several cases where it has jumped the fence and gone wild. It makes long-lived clumps and will tolerate alkaline soil.

seasons to reach flowering size. The freely produced seed will germinate easily if sown fresh, but seedlings can take five to seven years to reach flowering maturity.

The Martagons will thrive between shrubs, in light grass, or in open woodlands. At different times I have grown them in stiff clay, in alkaline soils, and in sandy areas, all with pleasing results. They do not seem to mind some shade but will not want heavy canopies, such as that provided by vigorous conifers. When planting them between shrubs, it is prudent to remember the rapid rate at which some can grow and be territorially greedy. Wherever *L. martagon* flourishes, you can expect the sturdy *L. hansonii* to be at least as happy and long-lived.

L. pardalinum is another long-term tenant, this kind being good between shrubs and in very light woodlands as well as in borders. The taller *L. pardalinum* var. *giganteum* can make impressive clumps with stems like a strong bamboo. Another American species that does well is *L. canadense,* which is a joy when it settles down and feels at home, but this and other species can be choosy.

Several Asian species can be naturalized. *L. davidii* does well between shrubs and in light woodlands, as will the tiger lily (*L. lancifolium*). But none can compare with *L. henryi* for determined longevity. I have it growing among viburnums, where the lily's leaning stems are supported, and here it produces heads of from six to a dozen orange blooms. It is not only tolerant of alkalinity but appears to relish it.

Hybrid lilies that are good for naturalizing are often those close to the species. 'Bright Star' has much of the *L. henryi* mode of growth in bulbs, stems, and shiny strong foliage. Its distinct flowers are wide stars, rather than the rolled-up balls of the species, and are white with deep honeyed centers. It was first offered for sale in 1957 and is still going strong. Other first-rate naturalizing plants are the hybrids of *L. pardalinum,* whose rhizomatous bulbs expand to form formidable stands. The color of these hybrids varies from golds to orange-reds, all with heavy spotting, sometimes heavily freckled. While many bulbs went out under the umbrella name of the Bellingham Group, a few clones were individually named, such as 'Shuksan', a tangerine-gold kind with black spots and the recurved tips of the petals dipped in red paint. The Bullwood Group are British-raised examples of these American species hybrids. 'Cherrywood' is a notable selection, its hanging heads having petals gently curved back but not to the tip-touching extent of the species.

The Martagon hybrids are a range of cultivars and seedlings bred mainly from crossing white and mauve forms of *L. martagon* with the thick-petaled, marmalade-colored *L. hansonii.* The first to be named was 'Marhan'—a neat combination of the parents' names—first recorded by the famous Dutch firm of Van Tubergen in 1891. Over a hundred years later, it shows no signs of weakening. The Citronella Group, first offered in 1958, is happily still with us. Its abundant pendent yellow blooms indicate the Asiatic species *L. davidii, L. amabile,* and *L. dauricum* in its parentage.

We approach the choosing of lilies with excitement but also with some trepidation. We are spoiled for choice, and each season brings many new kinds into the lists, so that the range of sizes, colors, and habits keeps expanding. The permutations are now endless.

choosing lilies

We will start by looking at the species, which form the more or less unchanging bedrock, though a few of the rarer and trickier ones tend to make only spasmodic appearances in lists of bulbs and seeds. To look at the species first will also give us a benchmark against which to measure the hybrids, since the breeders' work here has given us a deluge of

A few purists may decide to grow only species lilies, the kinds that have evolved through countless ages. Each species is likely to have become a plant of fairly tight specifications adapted to a certain environment, the dictates of the genome causing it to operate successfully only within prescribed limits. Some selected species can challenge gardeners but yet may find certain gardens to their liking and romp away. A more probable role is to titillate the desires of the masochists among us. Fortunately, most species are amenable to garden culture, though some may require attention to a specific need, such as a soil that is acidic rather than alkaline.

choosing lilies: the species

L. davidii (previous page), drawn rather more finely than the tiger lily, is an Asiatic species that stands some 3–4 feet tall, the arching stems having an usual complement of a dozen hanging flowers with raised purple dots.

L. duchartrei (opposite) is a plant with a strong nomadic inclination; its underground stems run about like youngsters in a playground, and along the stems new bulbs are formed. The pointed petals curve back to form Turk's caps, all white but usually intricately peppered purple-maroon.

Within a species there can be small but significant variations. You may find clones that fluctuate from the norm, especially in color, in spotting, in flower form, in habit, in optimum flower numbers, and, most importantly, in garden performance potential. An early instance of this is the selection of clones of *L. candidum* with full, wide-petaled flowers. In the wild, the plants are less well endowed, the flowers being smaller, less numerous, and noticeably more slender in the petal. Sometimes forms we are familiar with are clones that pass from garden to garden without reaching a commercial outlet; it makes good sense to join lily organizations where this freemasonry operates.

There is a useful clutch of wild lilies that make first-rate garden plants that can be grown without much fuss. Our aim is to mark the most reliable species, suggest others that are worth trying, and mention some others that could be worth the challenge of cultivation. Picking the most reliable, important species is akin to picking the world's all-time best baseball or football team: it can be fun but it can also be contentious, with everyone having a slightly different roll call. This is my lineup:
L. bulbiferum, L. candidum, L. monadelphum, L. hansonii, L. martagon, L. henryi, L. lancifolium, L. pardalinum, L. regale, and *L. speciosum.* Of these, the first three are classed as members of the Candidum group, the next two belong to the Martagons, while *L. henryi* and *L. lancifolium* are from the Asian group. This leaves *L. pardalinum* as the sole American member, *L. regale* the standard bearer for the Trumpets, and *L. speciosum* the solitary Oriental representative.

CLASSIFICATION
There are 80–100 accredited lily species. Nature does not provide us with labels and a classification, but botanists have suggested relationships between the various species that result in a number of groups, usually seven, which tend to be geographically delineated. Thus we have an Asian group, an American group, and an Oriental group. Other groups are defined by their similarity of form, such as the Trumpets, or their relationship to a dominant species, such as the Martagons. We follow Comber's classification of 1949, which has held sway for decades (see the Appendix, page 152).

the martagon group

L. martagon is one of the hardiest and most persistent of all the species. The illustration shows clearly the narrow cylindrical inflorescence as well as its typical "Turk's cap" flower form.

L. martagon, L. distichum, L. hansonii, L. medeoloides, L. tsingtauense
Characteristics: germination above-ground delayed, whorled leaves, jointed bulb scales (except *L. hansonii*), heavy seed, smooth petals, erect stems, relatively small flowers, and fruit as broad as long

Lilies of this group are found in China and Korea, with *L. martagon* being known in Siberia and all the way down to the Balkans; it also appears in different places across the southern half of Europe with a little less claim to indigenous status. In the wild it is the widest spread of all species. Plants can be found at sea level and at various heights up to 7,000 feet, and the soils in which it grows cover a wide pH spectrum from acid to alkaline. Among dedicated gardeners the martagon lily is a favorite. Once it has settled in, it is recognized as one of the most reliable and undemanding of species. There are plenty of gardens with populations of *L. martagon* over 50 years old and several with stands of more than double this age.

In several countries, way off its natural distribution, the freely produced seed has floated into the wild and colonies have been established. However, in the garden, bulbs that have been out of the ground for a while before being planted can sulk, and there may be no growth above ground for a complete year. But all is not lost—the bulb is unlikely to have disappeared. It will be rooting and getting ready to join the party the following year, and thereafter will be just as carefree as any. It makes good sense to try to obtain freshly dug bulbs.

Stems vary in height according to the clone, the age of the bulb, the garden conditions, and seasonal factors. Usually one can expect heights of 3–6 feet, but occasional individuals may outdo this. Most stronger stems will have three whorls of foliage, with 15 or more leaflets to each outward-pointing "platform." The number of flowers will vary from a modest half a dozen to several times this. Among my own plants are several with more than 35 blooms to a stem, and though 25 is a more common effort, one stem managed to reach 50. These flowers are held by shortish ascending flower stalks, so that the overall effect is of a column of bloom rather than a pyramid. The flowers are not huge and are formed of firm petals that curl back on themselves to form rounded hanging lanterns.

Colors vary from a pink-mauve standard to pale pink and very dark maroon. The darkest named form is *L. martagon* var. *cattaniae*, with its color being made more effective by the unusual lacquered finish—most Martagons use matte paint. Albinos are treasured; they shine out and help to highlight the other color shades. *L. martagon* var. *album* is usually a uniform snowy white but may be decorated with the spotting that is a feature of the colored forms. Pink spotting is typical of the white *L. martagon* var. *albiflorum*. The protruding anthers and stigmas add grace.

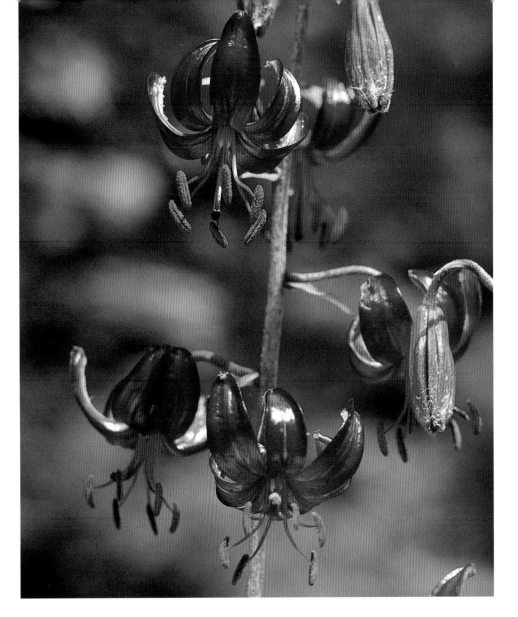

L. martagon **var.** *cattaniae* is a dark form characterized by its deep unspotted burgundy color, usually combined with a lacquered finish, and its hairy buds and stems.

L. martagon **var.** *album* is much sought after by gardeners on its own merits and for the contrast that it can create when planted near to *L. martagon*, with one highlighting the other. The white form is just as easy and long-lived as the type. Some are pure white, while others may have some small dark spots.

This species is extraordinarily free with its seed. One can harvest many pods from a stem, each full to bursting point, perhaps with up to 100 viable seeds. Sown fresh in the open or in pots in summer, the seed will germinate freely, but this is done surreptitiously underground in the following month, the first true leaves not appearing until into the new year. The plants will then grow steadily rather than dramatically; the bulbs reach flowering size in five to seven years.

One can be a little more adventurous in planting *L. martagon* than some others. Most lilies demand full sun and light to do well, but while the Martagons will be happy with this, they will also tolerate a moderate amount of shade, which means that they can be grown effectively between shrubs or in light woodland conditions. Most soils will support them well, but waterlogged ground is unsuitable.

It has been suggested by some botanists that the Martagon group species *L. hansonii* (see next page) is the closest to what is envisaged as the prototype from which the genus *Lilium* evolved, the most primitive features being the whorled foliage, recurved petals, yellow-orange flowers, erect strong stems, and bulbs of unjointed scales. In this last characteristic it differs from *L. martagon* itself.

OTHER SPECIES IN THIS GROUP ARE DESCRIBED ON PAGE 152.

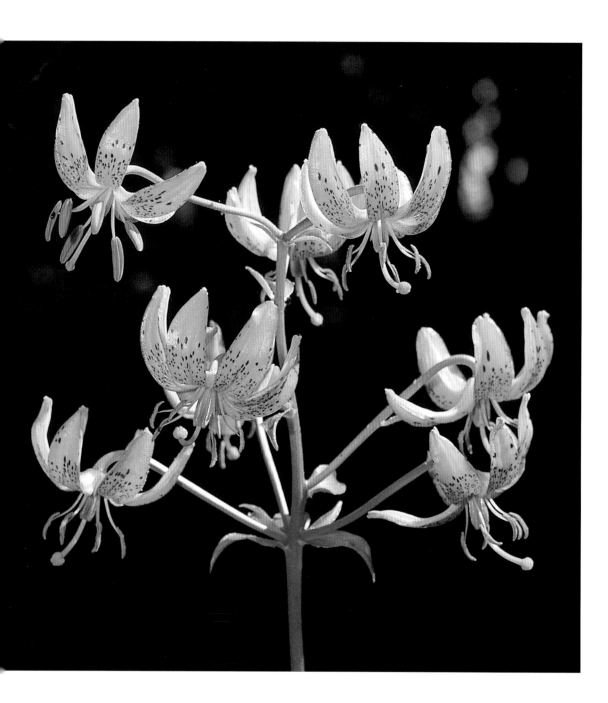

L. hansonii

L. hansonii is a splendid, sturdy plant in typical Martagon style, producing upright stems with whorls of leaves and heads of nodding flowers. These are made of recurving petals but not so curled up as its *L. martagon* relative. They are firmly textured and so thick with their orange coloring that it is easy to understand why a likeness to marmalade has been an almost standard metaphor.

Flowers are of a similar size to *L. martagon,* but with the petals being more widespread and the tips pointing upward, they can appear somewhat larger. The tangerine color is enlivened by spotting—if it were a child it would be nicknamed "Freckles." It stands 3–5 feet tall, and strong stem-rooting may help to engender the formation of bulblets on the underground stem. Once settled, the bulbs will increase steadily. It can be left *in situ* for as long as it is not too crowded by its own numbers or by the growth of other plants around. It needs an open site, perhaps between shrubs, in soil that is sufficiently open-structured as to be well-drained; it will tolerate some alkalinity in the soil.

L. tsingtauense

This distinctive lily from Korea and China is a robust plant, growing quickly from seed and making a reasonably behaved garden plant. It has typical erect stems with whorls of foliage, all in traditional Martagon style. However, it is the rebel of the family, as it displays its brash orange flowers gazing to the heavens and with the petals stretching out horizontally, with perhaps only the tips recurved. Each stem carries about five blooms. The majority of my plants have grown to around 2 feet tall, with an occasional one reaching toward 3 feet.

the north american group

a. *L. humboldtii, L. columbianum, L. kelloggii, L. washingtonianum, L. rubescens, L. bolanderi*
b. *L. pardalinum, L. nevadense, L. occidentale, L. maritimum, L. parvum, L. parryi,*
   L. vollmeri, L. wigginsii
c. *L. superbum, L. carolinianum, L. iridollae, L. michiganense, L. canadense, L. grayi*
d. *L. philadelphicum, L. catesbaei*

Charactersitics: germination above-ground delayed (except sometimes in *L. philadelphicum, L. parvum, L. parryi, L. humboldtii*), whorled leaves, jointed bulb scales (except section "a"), heavy seed (except section "c"), smooth petals, bulbs more or less rhizomatous and not erect, stems upright

Continentally isolated, with species often restricted to particular areas, this is a varied group of lilies. They are not necessarily easy plants to grow, but *L. pardalinum*, known as the leopard or panther lily, is normally reckoned as the most amenable of the group. It is found in the southern half of Oregon and hops down through California almost to the Mexican border. This is a very wide distribution area, which, as you might expect, is accompanied by some variation. The height of plants varies, as does the size of the brilliant hanging flowers—sufficiently for botanists of the splitting persuasion (who christen relatively unimportant variations) to give some populations the status of a variety or even a new species.

The standard *L. pardalinum* is a vigorous, upright plant with bright green stems and whorls of foliage. Flower heads of up to ten hanging buds or opened blooms are possible in midsummer, each petal being a golden tangerine color but with its tip dipped into crimson-vermilion paint. The tangerine is decorated with bold spots or splashes of deep maroon, this stronger coloring being more noticeable toward the base. Heads of half a dozen flowers are the norm, but since an established stand sends up plenty of stems, the total effect is very pleasing. Each bloom is formed of 3½ inches pointed petals, severely curled back to form individual arcs, thus emphasizing the protruding anthers and stigma. These anthers start life as long purple creations but quickly open to become golden with the revealed pollen. Heights vary from 3 to 6 feet, with most somewhere between these limits.

There is no better example of a rhizomatous lily bulb. The thick rootstock is amply supplied with yellow scales that tend to point out and up; the newer scales of the growing points start cream. Although the plants can be left for several years to get on with their own affairs, if you want to maximize the potential for increase, you can carefully lift part of the rootstock in late summer and divide off sections with a strong, sharp knife. Each portion will make an independent plant, provided it has one of the paler growing points. The injunction to lift "carefully" is prudent, for the waisted scales are brittle (see page 19), and you can easily find a distressing

L. pardalinum, the panther lily, is a trustworthy garden plant, thriving on neglect, and may well be chosen by most as the easiest of the American group of species. Characteristics are whorled foliage, pendent "Turk's cap" flowers, strong colors, heavy freckling, and rhizomatous bulbs.

L. superbum can rival *L. pardalinum* in strength and persistence. It is capable of forming considerable groups, with many stems and lots of bloom. It is usually several tones paler than the panther lily, but it can be a picture of exuberant health, with stems reaching to 8 feet in height.

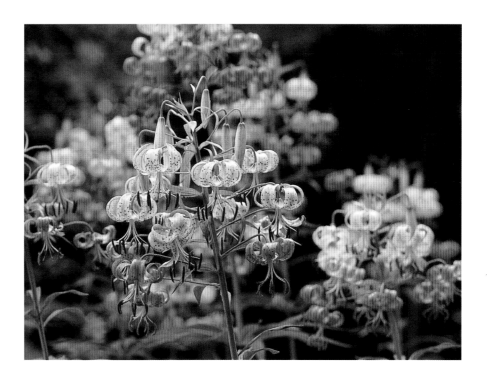

L. pardalinum **var.** *giganteum* is the first lily that I got to know, and I marveled at its prodigious vigor, producing plants then much taller than I—some 6 feet or so. It has a parade-ground stance with brilliant uniforms and is able to grow well even in soils that may initially look unpromising.

number of loose scales. If this happens, return the scales to the soil, as each has the potential to form a new plant, though it may take a few seasons to start flowering. *Lilium pardalinum* var. *giganteum* is either a particularly fine form or an early collected natural hybrid, possibly the result of an alliance with *L. humboldtii*. It is like the type but drawn much more boldly, its stems like bamboo stalks. Slightly larger blooms are possibly even more determinedly pendent and the flower colors of gold and crimson more precisely marked. Dark purple spots are very evident, sometimes ringed with yellow. Plants can grow strongly and soon form excellent stands. They do well in most soils, do not object to some alkalinity, and will manage in light shade.

    L. superbum is a vigorous plant, growing in the same manner as *L. canadense* (see page 49), with strongly stoloniferous bulbs supporting erect stems with whorled foliage. When settled and happy, it can sometimes have stems 9 feet high and plenty of them. Each will carry a quantity of sizeable flowers, which differ from its relative in having petals that curl back to make less distinctive ball-like blooms. The color is usually a pale tangerine, but this is variable, some being more yellow and others veering toward red, but there is invariably a generous sprinkling of large maroon dots. If this all sounds rather pedestrian against *L. canadense*, it does have the yeoman virtues of greater reliability and strength.

OTHER SPECIES IN THIS GROUP ARE DESCRIBED ON PAGES 152–53.

L. kelloggii (below)

In stature and form *L. kelloggii* is a half-sized relative of *L. pardalinum*, as if it were seen through the wrong end of a telescope. It usually measures 2–3 feet, though it is capable of reaching twice this. It has the same *L. pardalinum* or *L. martagon* style of growth, this time with ivory buds that open to take on a pinkish-mauve flush that deepens to purple before senescence. This is a good species that can do well in the garden. It also has a scent, something *L. pardalinum* lacks. The illustration is of a seedling of *L. kelloggii*—an alliance with a related species is suspected.

L. canadense (left)

Long known in cultivation—it was listed by Parkinson in 1629—*L. canadense* is considered a capricious plant. However, when it is doing well most fanciers would pick it as the most pleasing of all American species and perhaps of the genus. It produces a wonderful head of graceful blooms, with each flower hung out like a lantern on a 45-degree-angled pedicel; the petals describe a gentle arc that may just reach over the horizontal, a graceful classic pose. The color varies from gold to deep orange, with occasional red forms. The stoloniferous bulbs can grow strongly and divide steadily; they need deep soil, free of alkalinity.

L. grayi (above)

This is a dainty and distinct species whose smallish, rhizomatous bulbs support relatively strong, erect stems some 3–5 feet high. The bells are held at a tilt below the horizontal on longish pedicels that are often at a 45-degree angle. The petals form a true bell and then open toward the mouth. All is a rich orange-red, the inside being more golden but well endowed with dark beauty spots. Half a dozen flowers to a stem is a modest score.

the candidum group

L. candidum is endemic to the Balkans and the Middle East. Known as the Madonna lily, it has a history of association with human civilization that long precedes the birth of Christ. Utility and beauty are combined in this plant. It was used early on as a fodder plant, the bulbs being edible, but it was also chosen to provide floral décor for funerals and other occasions.

L. candidum, L. chalcedonicum, L. pomponium, L. carniolicum, L. pyrenaicum, L. ciliatum, L. monadelphum, L. polyphyllum, L. bulbiferum

Characteristics: germination below-ground (except *L. bulbiferum*, *L. polyphyllum, L. monadelphum*), delayed (except rarely *L. candidum*), scattered leaves, many entire bulb scales, heavy seed, Turk's cap flowers (except *L. candidum, L. bulbiferum*), erect stems, normally no stem roots

This group is basically European but ventures into the Middle East and the Republic of Georgia. *L. candidum* stands aloof; *L. monadelphum* is fairly close botanically. On the whole, none of the species in this group provides insuperable difficulties in cultivation.

The Madonna lily heads the team despite its vulnerability to virus. There can be few sights more impressive than a healthy stand of *L. candidum* in full bloom. It will be manufacturing scent, and each bell rings out a benison of idealized beauty, an echo of the impression made through the centuries as a revered monastery garden plant, a specimen in the botanic collection, or a cottage garden favorite. It still holds some of the aura of the ideal cottage garden flower, although it is now much less widely grown. It blooms in early summer, with the stronger bulbs capable of having up to 20 flowers on stems up to 5 feet high, but it is more usual to have pleasing stems of a dozen flowers hoist up some 4 feet. The flowers face outward and are held close to the stem to make the beginning of a column. "Candidum" means sparkling white, and this they certainly are, though there is a touch of gold in the center, and the anthers are a rich yellow.

Almost uniquely in the genus, the bulbs make a rosette of long oval leaves after the flowering stem dies away, and this useful ground marker is kept through the winter—an evergreen lily. With the spring, the stem shoots up from the center with alternate or scattered leaves that are relatively broad and kept close to the stem, but getting smaller as they mount the stem. This is a plant to grow in an open, sunny spot. Alone in the genus, it is a lily to plant shallowly, with the noses of the bulbs just under the soil surface. Planting time is a few weeks after blooming, toward the end of summer. It does best in open, well-drained soil that has some alkalinity. Once planted, it is best left undisturbed until obviously overcrowded, after a few years.

This lily's susceptibility to virus makes it prudent to grow it as far away from other lilies as is possible. The contrast between healthy plants and those debilitated by virus is a salutary lesson. Try to get virus-free stock, which can be raised commercially from the tiny growing center of the bulb, the meristem; this is grown on, propagated, and eventually marketed. Seed may be available but is sometimes only sparsely produced; plants raised from seed will start life free from disease.

L. bulbiferum var. _croceum_
is the best-known form of a species named for its habit of forming bulbils in its leaf axils. Unfortunately, this form does not follow the type's lead, but even without the bulbils the bulbs are strong and increase easily. It is one of the earlier lilies to bloom and is a trouble-free plant.

Virus may be suspected if the foliage has streaks of paler coloration, often giving a yellowish cast to the whole. Badly infected plants can have distorted foliage and flowers. There is no cure, so all parts of the attacked plants should be destroyed; to leave a diseased one will invite aphids to spread the infection. Other causes of failure could be long periods in waterlogged soils, or bulbs planted much too deeply.

One of the most important species in this group is _L. bulbiferum_, a key plant in the breeding of Asiatic hybrids. This is a European species native to the Pyrenees, and spreading through the Alps, and somewhat to the north. It is a flamboyant, upward-facing, widespread flower in brilliant orange-red. It is variable in color, but the standard is a bright orange that deepens to red toward the petal tips. Raised spots are painted deep chocolate-maroon, a color that can appear again towards the flower centers. The usual form found nowadays is _L. bulbiferum_ var. _croceum_, similarly spotted but a more or less uniform orange. The wide bells open to become almost flat. This form and the species itself were used to produce the series marketed as _L. × hollandicum_ (_L. bulbiferum_ × _L. maculatum_) as early as 1879. This was the launch-pad for the modern Asiatic hybrids, _L. bulbiferum_ being the cuckoo in the nest as the only European species involved in their breeding.

While somewhat in the shade of its descendants, _L. bulbiferum_ is a strong garden plant that grows quickly in spring to bloom at the start of summer, which makes it one of the first to open. It stands 3 feet tall, and while normally happy with six or eight flowers, it has been recorded with several times as many. Polished, medium-green leaves are held away from the stem. It seems to do best if dug up at the end of summer, split, and replanted in a fresh spot. Below ground, the stems will be found to be energetically rooting. The specific name acknowledges the ability of the type to produce bulbils in the leaf axils, although some clones, like _L. bulbiferum_ var. _croceum_, lack this characteristic. The nearest hybrid to the species is 'Orange Triumph'

OTHER SPECIES IN THIS GROUP ARE DESCRIBED ON PAGE 153.

L. pyrenaicum

This is a welcome lily in any collection, as it will probably be the first to bloom outside. Its very leafy stems can be topped by nodding buds and flowers as early as late spring. Bulbs are formed of many narrow scales. They can take a little while to settle; but once established, they will begin to form clumps that will last for years. The flowers are quite crowded, pendent Turk's caps in lime-tinted gold with lots of dark spots. The species has tended to receive a bad press on account of the unpleasant smell of the flowers, but this can usually be detected only by someone determined to get their nose among them. Like most Europeans, it will tolerate alkaline soil.

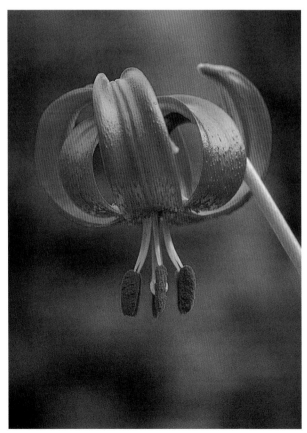

L. chalcedonicum

A familiar plant in the garden of my childhood, this is now rare in cultivation, possibly due to a predisposition to virus disease. It is a showy kind of lily, growing to 3–5 feet its stems well clothed with scattered leaves that are relatively broad and held quite close to the stem. Three to a dozen pendent Turk's cap flowers make rather close heads, their brilliant vermilion accentuated by a high-gloss finish. The standard form is spotless, but the rather more vigorous *L. chalcedonicum* var. *maculatum* bears a few spots. With *L. candidum*, this is a parent of the accidental hybrid *L.* × *testaceum*.

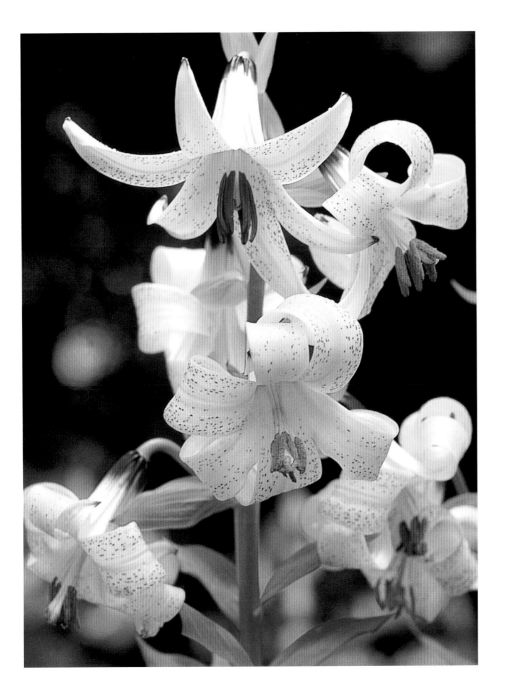

L. monadelphum

Bulbs of this lily are found growing wild in the Caucasus, often in such large numbers as to turn hillsides yellow. The flowers are nodding, with wide petals that curl back. What is taken as the type is a somewhat darker shade than the form long cultivated as *L. szovitsianum*, which is a rich primrose with anthers of rusty orange, rather than the yellow of the type. The bulbs are large and composed of many narrow scales. They can take a little while really to settle after being planted but, once established, they last for many decades. Stems can be expected to reach 2–5 feet, depending on their position, with polished, broad, arching foliage and heads of five or so open bells of recurved, wide petals. There are usually a few tiny chocolate spots. Individual flowers are as large as those of the Madonna lily, so a head makes a fine picture and a group something even more so.

The plants thrive in a wide variety of soils, and they are alkalinity tolerant. I have grown them on very heavy clay and in silty soils equally well. They normally give lots of seed, and this will germinate well, though the seedlings may take five years or longer to reach flowering size. If they are grown individually in pots and planted out after two seasons, the waiting period is reduced to the minimum. Bulbs should be left undisturbed in a sunny, open spot; if they must be moved, do this in mid- to late summer. *L. kesselringianum* is a slightly anorexic version of this species, paler and with narrower petals.

the oriental group

L. speciosum, L. auratum, L. nobilissimum, L. japonicum, L. rubellum, L. brownii
Characteristics: germination above-ground delayed (except a form of
L. brownii and, rarely, L. speciosum), scattered leaves with distinct leaf stalk,
entire bulb scales, trumpet flowers (except L. auratum, L. speciosum), erect
bulbs, white (except some forms of L. speciosum)

This is a group of Japanese and Far Eastern lilies. They enjoy open, acid soils and can flourish in gardens free from violent fluctuations of temperature and moisture, but may be shorter-lived than lilies in other groups. They are enticingly beautiful.

L. speciosum is a leading member of this select group, a species that many may think the choicest of a massively endowed genus. It is one of the latest to bloom, often opening at summer's end, but the flowers last well, the half-dozen or more on a stem giving a pleasing succession. Each semi-pendent bloom is hung out on a long pedicel, so that there is plenty of air around—a most graceful pose. Petals are curved back and are marked with a generous number of raised points, or papillae, often more richly painted than the usual crimson-pink of the major part. The strength of coloring lessens toward the margins, which can be

L. speciosum from Japan is arguably the most graceful of a genus full of grace. It cannot tolerate the slightest alkalinity in the soil. It is this species crossed with *L. auratum* that has produced the enormously varied and opulent Oriental hybrids.

L. speciosum var. *album* is the pristine, snowy-white form of the species. It would be a delight at any time, but blooming as it does at the very end of the lily season, it is especially welcome.

white. There are many gradations of color; pure white clones are ethereal, but most have some warm pink coloring, and there are others painted a rich crimson. The golden-green nectary grooves are noticeable, while dark pollen makes a decorative feature of the anthers. This is all in a cloud of perfume over the wiry stems and long, stalked, spear-shaped leaves. The foliage is pleasing in itself. This species can be grown successfully outdoors in gardens with neutral or acid soil. There are parts of America, Australia, and New Zealand where it romps away— perhaps even more so than in its native Japan! It makes a wonderful plant for containers, with the virtue of coming into bloom after many others are just a memory.

L. speciosum var. *gloriosoides* is obviously close to *L. speciosum* in growth and habit, but it has very distinctive blooms. The wide flowers—four or so to a stem— have wavy-margined petals spreading widely before recurving, and facing outward rather than being pendent, like *L. speciosum*. The white flowers have conspicuous green nectaries and many crimson spots toward the center of each petal, while the dark anthers are conspicuously arranged in front of the blooms. This lily has all the modesty of a can-can dancer. Plants stand 2–3 feet tall and grow as easily as any of the rest of the group in non alkaline, open soils.

OTHER SPECIES IN THIS GROUP ARE DESCRIBED ON PAGE 153.

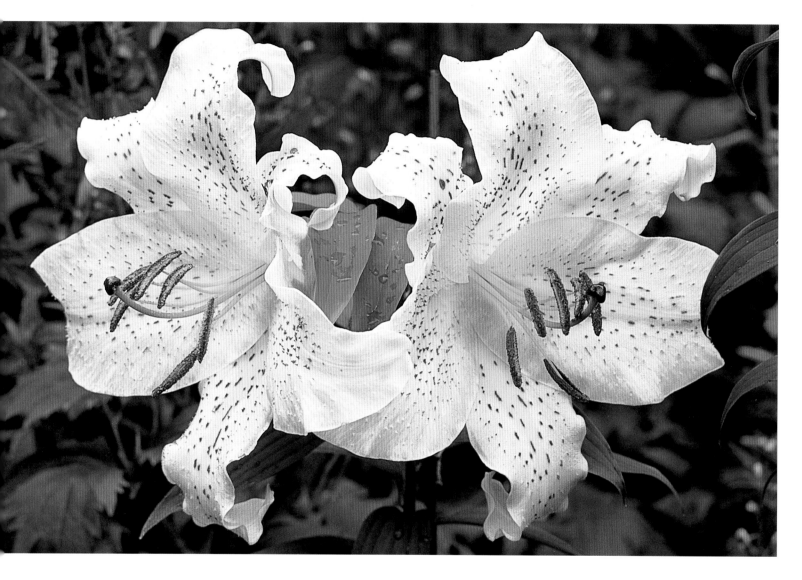

L. auratum

This is the Japanese species that caused a sensation when first shown in London in July 1862. Thereafter, millions were collected from their homes on the slopes of extinct volcanoes, where they grew in the volcanic ash. Growers tended to force-feed the bulbs, something the plants did not necessarily enjoy. And while the plant may have appeared to flourish, it could be that it was relying more on the extensive stem roots than on those of the bulb, which, when lifted at the end of the season, may have been a miserable wasted item or have completely rotted away.

Flowers can be 8–10 inches across, wide bowls facing outward. Each white petal can be 6 inches long and is usually marked with a central yellow stripe to justify its common name, gold-banded lily. Crimson spotting is frequent. In some there is a strong suffusion of crimson in place of much of the golden stripe, and the main parts of the petals are blushing pink. The perfume is almost overpowering.

Bulbs need an open, neutral to acid soil that may have some rotted organic material added. Additional mulches can encourage stem-rooting. Nowadays the species is less widely grown than the many hybrids originally derived from crossing this with *L. speciosum*; these have taken over all decorative duties and are much easier plants.

L. rubellum

This is another Japanese species, a beauty but tantalizingly awkward in cultivation. In growth it is similar to *L. speciosum*, but the flowers are distinct. At their bases they are narrowly trumpet-shaped but at the mouth the petals expand widely. Stems can be 12–30 inches tall and carry one to five blooms, which are usually a most pleasing uniform rich rose-pink. This color can vary a little, with some flowers being paler. Bulbs need excellent drainage, especially in the winter, and would seem to do best in a compost rich in leaf mold.

the asian group

a. *L. duchartrei, L. lankongense, L. papilliferum, L. davidii, L. leichtlinii, L. lancifolium, L. henryi, L. rosthornii*

b. *L. concolor, L. callosum, L. fargesii, L. cernuum, L. pumilum, L. amabile*

c. *L. amoenum, L. exanthum, L. henricii, L. mackliniae, L. nanum, L. paradoxum, L. sempervivoideum, L. sherriffiae, L. soulieli, L. bakerianum, L. wardii, L. taliense, L. nepalense, L. primulinum, L. ochraceum*

Characteristics: germination below-ground immediate (except *L. henryi*), scattered leaves, entire bulb scales, light seed (except *L. henryi, L. amabile*), Turk's cap flowers, erect bulbs, white (except *L. henryi* and some of section "c"), stems more or less stoloniform (except section "b"), stem-rooting, stigma small
a. petals and nectary papilliferous, nectary with hairs, seed winged
b. few bulb scales, erect stems, 2 stems from single nose bulb, seed wingless
c. smooth petals, hairless nectary, seed winged

L. henryi is one of the most reliable and most persistent of garden lilies; it will perform for decades with little attention. In areas where alkaline soil is so prevalent, it is valued for its high tolerance of this kind of soil, and it has been used in breeding many hybrids with this trait.

The Asian lilies are a diverse group, ranging from tiny plants to giants, and, similarly, some can be the easiest of garden characters, while others can challenge the skills of the most dedicated growers. On occasion gardens have been untended for several years allowing shrubs to burgeon out of control and scrub with energetic weeds to make serious bids for command. *L. henryi* may have been growing in civilized conditions only to have become hopelessly overgrown—the bulbs perhaps imagining themselves to be back in their native Asian homelands. They appeared to have been lost altogether, but when the ground was cleared, the bulbs came quickly back into their own and began to produce their familiar arching stems with polished leaves and heads of hanging flowers. It said a lot for the stamina of these plants.

L. henryi is classified with others of the large Asian group, but it is one of the most distinct and gives the impression of being one of the more primitive species. Its bulbs are large, sometimes massive. Strong stems can be 4–8 feet long, well clothed with long, broad, arching leaves in rich green and may be carrying a considerable load of flowers. Wild plants may have to be satisfied with only one to four blooms to a stem, but under cultivation they produce more—6 to 12 is ordinary—and stems have been known with more than 30. The large flowers tend to look downward, their petals strongly recurved as they open and mature. They reveal an inner surface much decorated by what looks like a dermatological eruption—large numbers of pimples (papillae), dominating the petals' lower halves.

The flower color is medium-orange with some darker spots, likely to fade slightly in strong sunlight. The plants do not object to light shading, and this helps prevent too dramatic a bleaching. The nectary channels are clearly marked in green down the center base of each petal, the total resulting in a star motif in the center of each bloom. Plants come into flower considerably later than the majority of lilies—in late summer, after most of the Asian group but not usually as late as

L. lancifolium var. *flaviflorum* is the rare yellow form of the tiger lily, long previously known as *L. tigrinum*. This easy lily has a habit of producing lots of bulbils in the leaf axils, an almost excessively generous means of procreation.

L. speciosum. This plant is looked to with gratitude by breeders, who give thanks for its huge input into the breeding of modern hybrids, first by crossing with the Trumpet *L. sargentiae* to produce the Aurelian hybrids, and then to enter conjugal relations with the Orientals to give us a new race of fantastic flowers that tolerate alkaline soils—the "Orienpets." The species is also little affected by virus—its inherent strength would seem to resist it or at least mask its effects. Fresh stock can be raised from seed.

Hailing from the same habitat as *L. henryi*, central China, *L. rosthornii* is botanically close to this species and may be a form of it. It differs in having longer, narrower leaves, long seedpods, and flowers marked by more distinct spots.

Lilies have their fair share of synonyms, but on the whole these cause little confusion. With *L. lancifolium*, it seems wise to include its former name, *L. tigrinum*, as this is still widely remembered and echoes its common name, the tiger lily. This is one of the easiest of lilies to grow and may be the one that first makes an impact with children, who can be fascinated by its habit of producing babies "up the stem." Each leaf axil can have one or more dark bulbils, so that a single stem may be the progenitor of an army. Left to themselves, some of the bulbils will start to produce roots and small leaves before they naturally fall to the ground. Here the roots pierce the soil and, taking a hold on it, pull the bulb down by contracting accordian-wise. Larger bulbils can result in plants that will flower in a couple of seasons. This useful method of propagation can be inherited by its hybrid offspring.

This robust species has wiry, dark stems and lots of narrow, dark, arching leaves. Its extrovert attitude to life can hold a disadvantage. A bulb that is attacked with virus can persist for many years, and the symptoms of the attack are not always noticed, the paler stripes of the leaves not being very obvious. All the bulbils picked off such a plant will be infected with the virus, and the same virus transmitted to other kinds of lily can affect these much more virulently.

A healthy stand of tiger lilies can be most impressive. The purple-black, rigidly upright stems, 5–6 feet tall and clothed with the arching foliage, make an ideal background for the many bright orange-red flowers hung out to attract attention. It is possible to have 25–35 flowers on a stem, and, since each bloom can be 4 inches across, heavily decorated with dark spots, the total effect is inspiring.

In its native China the bulbs of *L. lancifolium* have long been valued as a food. It spread to Korea and Japan, and over time, the more robust forms have been selected. This has favored "triploid" forms, usually offered for sale to gardeners, which seem to manage in all soils, including those with some alkalinity. Another form, *L. lancifolium* var. *splendens*, is a richer red, slightly larger, its spots painted with a bolder brush. A double form, *L. lancifolium* 'Flore Pleno', loses some of its sexual parts to the formation of extra petals—not an exercise that I find altogether praiseworthy.

OTHER SPECIES IN THIS GROUP ARE DESCRIBED ON PAGES 153–54.

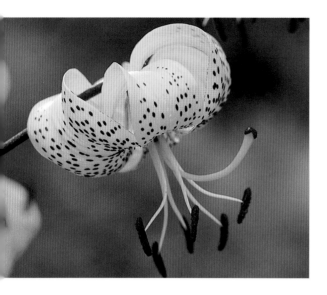

L. leichtlinii (above)

A less ebullient plant than the tiger lily but an engaging one in flower, with bright lemon or golden hanging blooms, well decorated with dark spots. This is now thought to be a form of the stronger kind, *L. leichtlinii* var. *maximowiczii*, with a rich red flower, though each retains its official status at present. They are both smaller in flower than the tiger lily, have hairless stems, and do not produce stem bulbils. They grow easily from seed.

L. mackliniae (below)

An enchanting lily when growing well, it seems to do best in cooler climates such as the Pacific Northwest, for example. Usually rather low growing, it can bloom on stems only 6 inches high but when thriving may reach up to 30 inches, with narrow, dark leaves more or less at right angles to the erect stems. Smaller bulbs with dwarf stems may be happy with a single bell, but stronger stems can have six or more. The hanging mauve- pink buds swing up somewhat as the cup-shaped flowers open; petals are concave with only the tips recurving slightly outward. Color inside is white or palest blush-pink. Altogether a graceful and engaging character, it is unfortunately prone to the debilitating effects of virus. However, it is not difficult to raise from fresh seed, and where the plant grows at all reasonably, it is always prudent to have backup stock being raised from seed.

L. lankongense

This is a delightful species with slender stems reaching 3–4 feet or more. Foliage is narrow and plentiful. Flowers are pendent and recurved, somewhat akin to those of *L. duchartrei* (see page 41), but the buds are a pinkish mauve, and flowers open to reveal pink petals generously decorated with purple-red spots.

This coloring is variable in intensity, but there is always an inclination toward the lilac or mauve range rather than the yellowish pinks. Some dozen or more curled flowers are daintily displayed in well-spaced heads.

In cool, moist soils it can be somewhat easier to grow than some species, though in my own dry garden, while seed germinates readily, it has not proved very easy to establish, any temporary foothold being soon lost.

L. nepalense

One of the most dramatic species of the genus and now widely available. The bulbs send out stoloniferous stems dedicated to a nomadic life; they may travel far away from their mother before breaking into the airspace above. Then they make stems up to about 30 inches high but usually well within this limit. Quite broad foliage is more or less alternately arranged below the extraordinarily large blooms, usually one or two to a stem. These flowers expand widely from the base— trumpet-bowls colored a pale lime-cream on the outward-pointing petal tips but very boldly painted over at least two-thirds of the central surfaces in an unparalleled deep purple-maroon that has a slightly lacquered finish. This is perhaps made a little more obvious by gentle longitudinal corrugations.

L. taliense (left)
Rather like a big brother to *L. duchartrei* (see page 41), this has up to a dozen scented, white Turk's caps hung from strong stems 4–6 feet high. The white is peppered with little dark purple spots, and sometimes the whole is suffused with a suggestion of mauve-pink. The plentiful foliage is narrow and scattered. Most, but not all, clones have bulbs with stoloniferous stems, but it is not in the same walkabout league as
L. duchartrei. This species is rare in cultivation.

L. wardii (right)
When growing strongly this can have stems 5 feet high carrying 25–35 pink-mauve blooms fashioned in the Martagon mode. The nectary is marked in purple. Lesser stems may reach only 3 feet and carry two or three flowers. The plants enjoy humus and with this they can tolerate some lime. Stoloniferous stems engender new bulbs but fresh seed germinates easily and seedlings can grow quickly to flowering size (within two seasons).

the trumpet group

a. *L. sargentiae, L. sulphureum, L. leucanthum, L. regale*
b. *L. longiflorum, L. neilgherrense, L. formosanum, L. philippinense, L. wallichianum*
  Characteristics: germination below-ground immediate, scattered leaves with no leaf stalks, entire bulb scales, light seed (except *L. regale, L. longiflorum, L. neilgherrense*), trumpet-shaped flowers, erect bulbs, large stigma, stem roots
  a. bulbs dark purple or brown
  b. bulbs white, flowers large and narrow

The Trumpet group, from China, India, and the Pacific islands, is formed of some glorious species—everybody's idea of the perfect lily. *L. regale*, the most famous and successful Trumpet species in the garden, is a strong midsummer-flowering plant that does well in most soils and most climates. But some of the later-flowering kinds, while beautiful, often fall prey to virus diseases quite quickly.

L. regale has held its place as one of the most popular of all garden bulbs. It can produce very large heads of flowers that are rich purple-maroon in bud and sparkling white when open, but with rich golden bases. Their size is considerable and the scent powerful. Seed is produced freely, and this can be converted into bulbs able to produce a flower in a couple of seasons on a stem less than 2 feet high. As the bulbs grow larger, the stems carry more flowers, perhaps as many as 20–30 on stems reaching up to 6 feet tall. It does well both in the open ground and in containers—the larger, the better. Its energy is apparent in the early start it makes into growth, but this makes it vulnerable to damage from a late frost. Neighboring plants will afford some protection, shrubs may shelter it from the worst frost, and, as a last resort, early growth can be covered with a frost-protection blanket after a frost warning. Then all should be well.

OTHER SPECIES IN THIS GROUP ARE DESCRIBED ON PAGE 154.

L. regale celebrates its hundred years in cultivation. Most gardeners will agree that this is the outstanding introduction of the leading plant collector Ernest Wilson, who managed to find and bring into cultivation a fantastic number of fine plants.

L. regale var. ***album*** is the pure white form of the species. It lacks the rosy-purple bud color but is similar in all other respects. Both forms flower in midsummer.

L. longiflorum

The Easter lily is one of the most familiar of all the genus by virtue of its wide use as a cut flower. Though not completely hardy, it can be grown in the open in warmer parts of the world and under glass elsewhere. Greenish-ivory buds open to pure white trumpets, narrow at the base but widely expanded at the mouth. It is heavily textured and highly fragrant. Seed sown in early spring under glass and well grown can result in autumn blooms. Still a leading pot plant, it is now one of the parents of the important LAs, hybrids between this species and Asiatic cultivars.

L. leucanthum var. centifolium

This is the usual representative of the rare species
L. leucanthum, and one that has been extensively used in
breeding. It is a chaste, massive white trumpet, with petals
opening generously at the mouth and throats widely painted
in gold. It can be fall before the large purple buds open to
reveal pure white trumpets with anthers holding rusty red
pollen. The stems grow to 4–7 feet high.

We now turn to the hybrids to give some idea of the way modern cultivars have evolved, as well as to highlight some beautiful and reliable kinds. There is a steady turnover of cultivars, especially among the Asiatics, but that should not daunt us. If a particular cultivar falls out of the lists either temporarily or permanently, there will be others of similar or slightly better specifications waiting to be tried. There may, in fact, be a temptation to choose the newer cultivars. After all, new lilies will have been chosen for propagation and marketing only after careful appraisal of the distinctiveness of their overall appearance and/or performance.

choosing lilies: the hybrids

'Acapulco', one of a legion of Oriental hybrids, is imbued with all the glamour of the East in opulent form, exotic color, and heavenly perfume. A floral fantasy, it is as perfectly groomed as a geisha girl and has long been considered the best of the upright pink Orientals. Here it is shown almost twice its actual size.

Any emphasis on the novelties should not preclude the claims of some of the older kinds. There are many lily hybrids well over 50 years old that can hold their own in the competitive border and yet others reaching toward their centenaries that seem as vigorous as ever and still well worth growing. Trumpet lilies such as the Pink Perfection Group were produced around 1950 and introduced a decade later. Golden Splendor Group was introduced in 1957, while the African Queen Group made its debut the following year. The Bellingham Group, bred from wild American species, predates all these, being first listed in 1933. Of deliberately engendered hybrids, the most venerable is probably the Martagon hybrid 'Marhan', dating from 1891.

There are important points to be made, first about the overall value of hybrids and secondly about their availability. Almost invariably, the hybrids will be easier plants to grow than the species, since breeders have consistently selected the better performers. The process of crossbreeding the original species quickly ensured that many, if not all, of the inhibitions of a particular species were canceled out by the genetic input of other kinds. The success of the Asiatic hybrids is a classic example (see page 74). Perhaps the most significant of influences traceable to a single species is the blood donated by *L. henryi* when linked to that of the Trumpets and the alkalinity-intolerant Orientals. The race derived from Orientals crossed with *L. henryi* or one of its hybrids has given us exotics such as 'Black Beauty' and 'Scheherazade', with a tolerance of alkaline soil.

The second point to be made about our hybrids is that all named lilies are going to be good, but there is a constant inflow of new lilies that will not be mentioned here. In different parts of the world, the selection of available new lilies is likely to vary, though there will be many common to all markets. Where certain kinds are not listed, there will be a range of look-alikes to choose from. The influx of new lilies is particularly fast among the LA hybrids, which have rapidly become an important feature of the cut-flower trade, but the standard Asiatics and the Orientals are similarly active in procreation.

early hybrids: clones and series

'Mrs. R. O. Backhouse', from *L. hansonii* × *L. martagon*, was given an Award of Merit in 1921. It is a pale maize-yellow with a hint of pink and just lightly dotted.

NOTE: Where known, the date of introduction and the parentage of a cultivar are given in the caption.

Sometimes wild lilies are visited by insects bearing alien pollen, and this may result in hybrid seed. The same thing happens under cultivation, and some of these accidental hybrids have played an important role in gardens.

One of the most famous early hybrids was raised at the beginning of the nineteenth century in Holland or Germany. It was named *L.* × *testaceum* by Dr. John Lindley when it was illustrated in the Botanical Register of 1842, and its parentage is recorded as *L. chalcedonicum* × *L. candidum*. It has beautiful flowers standing as high as the taller parent, the Madonna lily, and with similar foliage but with hanging flowers of a very pleasing, soft, creamy orange. The blooms are large and wide, though the petal tips recurve, and the bright orange pollen contrasts with the paler flower color. Bulbs were widely distributed for many decades, but many eventually succumbed to virus disease. Once the technology was available, however, fresh clean stock was raised by meristem culture, and *L.* × *testaceum* is still a plant well worth growing. There are still only a limited number of *L. candidum* hybrids, of which 'Limerick' is one; this pale creamy flower of pendent pose opens early and grows with ease. But there are significantly more hybrids arising from *L. martagon*.

In the nineteenth century it was the fashion to give hybrids a botanical, Latinized name, as for the species, whether it was originally a single clone such as *testaceum* or a range of seedlings such as × *hollandicum* or × *dalhansonii*. Nowadays a group of plants of similar origin may be given a non-Latin colloquial name, such as Pink Perfection Group. To distinguish a cultivar from a group in print, all cultivar names are enclosed in single quotation marks—for example, 'Enchantment'. Most lily cultivars are single clones. Group names, on the other hand, will be unadorned—for example, Golden Splendor Group.

martagon hybrids

In 1891 the mating of *L. martagon* var. *album* with *L. hansonii* gave the Dutch firm of Van Tubergen the cultivar 'Marhan', the name being a combination of those of the parents. 'Marhan' is a true cultivar, a single clone that has been vegetatively increased for over a century without losing its vigor. The cross was repeated elsewhere equally successfully. All the hybrids from the mating of these two species are gathered together under the series name *L.* × *dalhansonii*, named around 1890, the original clone being from *L. martagon* var. *dalmaticum* × *L. hansonii*, a chestnut-brown flower with golden spots.

One of the earliest plant-breeding partnerships was that of Mr. and Mrs. R. O. Backhouse at their home, Sutton Court, in the village of Sutton St. Nicholas, near Hereford, England. Their garden saw the birth of many fine daffodils as well as lilies. Especially successful were the *L. martagon* × *L. hansonii* alliances, such as 'Mrs R. O. Backhouse'. A similar hybrid, 'Sutton Court', was featured in the *Gardener's Chronicle* in 1925. I saw it growing at Sutton Court, where it was found after decades of neglect when a descendant of the original Backhouse family returned from working as a geneticist in Argentina, where he had raised outstandingly successful strains of wheat. The plants at Sutton Court had been covered with thick tangles of brambles but managed to survive.

Among other martagon hybrids, 'Ellen Willmott' is thought to be a seedling from 'Marhan'; it is somewhat paler. 'Theodore Haber' was bred from the dark *L. martagon* var. *cattaniae* × *L. tsingtauense*. Its rich coloring is enhanced by the high-laquer finish.

'Komet B' is a robust plant with dark stems and neat whorls of foliage topped by good heads of curled pendent blooms in a vibrant deep orange. The pose is orthodox Martagon style, but the color would seem to have been inherited from a plant such as *L. tsingtauense*.

hybrids of american species

These are not numerous, which is a pity, as they make excellent garden plants for places where they can be left growing for a long time. They are ideal naturalizing subjects, growing well between shrubs, in light woodland conditions, and in borders. The Bellingham Group was introduced in the early 1930s, though the first work was done as long ago as 1918 in Los Angeles. The initial hybrids were from the crosses *L. parryi* × *L. ocellatum* and *L. pardalinum* × *L. ocellatum*. Those with *L. pardalinum* blood were the strongest and became dominant. Somewhat later, *L. humboldtii, L. bolanderi,* and *L. kelloggii* were added to the genetic stew, and the colors ranged from a clear yellow to bright orange-red, with most well-spotted dark brown. Of the few named clones, one of the best was 'Shuksan', which is still being grown.

Derek Fox, in Hockley, Essex, England, produced a fine range of hybrids from *L. pardalinum* × a pink 'Henry Bolander' hybrid ('Henry Bolander' was from *L. pardalinum* × *L. bolanderi*). This range was called the Bullwood Group and contained apricot, peach, tangerine, and red flowers. They were pendent, with recurved petals generously dotted. A particularly good selection from these was 'Cherrywood' (1964), a tall plant with widely spaced flowers of rich gold and very deep red. The petals sweep outward and point up but are not reflexed in the exaggerated form of *L. pardalinum*. They look very dainty and pleasing.

'Lake Tahoe' (1977) is dark crimson-pink for more than half of each petal from the tip, but has a white gold-banded center and a green nectary; there are dark pink-red spots. This is considered by Edward McRae, the breeder, to be clearly the best of the American species hybrids.

'Shuksan' (1933) is a strong plant with flowers mainly a rich gold, boldly spotted, with the tips of the petals touched with crimson; it grows 4–6 feet tall. (*L. humboldtii* × *L. pardalinum*)

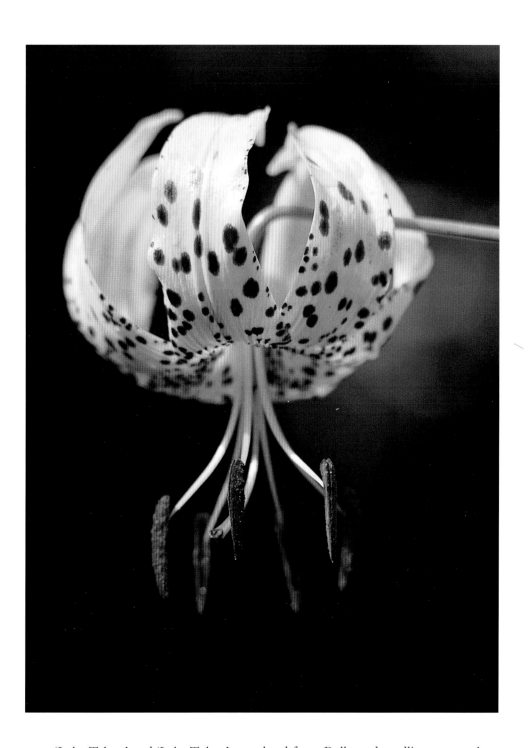

'Lake Tahoe' and 'Lake Tulare' were bred from Bullwood seedlings crossed with *L. bolanderi*. Both cultivars stand 6–8 feet tall. 'Lake Tulare' is a widely curved flower with its petals pointed up, in which maroon pink coloring gives way to white, gold, and green. The long pedicels of these pendent flowers ensure that they are well displayed.

popular asiatic hybrids

'Connecticut King' (1967) is a strong plant that for decades was a dominant cultivar in the cut-flower market but also prized in the garden. Strong golden flowers just slightly more strongly colored toward the center are combined with healthy bright and shiny green foliage. ('Connecticut Lass' × 'Keystone')

In the breeding of the Asiatic hybrids the story gets complicated, with more kinds of lily being involved. It is thought that natural hybrids had been collected by Japanese cultivators for some centuries before Europeans were allowed entry to the country. The Japanese have long been patient horticultural craftspeople and connoisseurs. Close proximity in gardens would have brought about further hybridization, resulting in a series of red and orange flowers. How far this was sheer chance or conscious manipulation is a matter for speculation.

Thunberg was one of the first foreigners allowed into the closed country of Japan. He managed to get a series of lilies away to Europe, where they were known as *L. × thunbergianum* or *L. × elegans*. However, the name *L. × maculatum* was first officially used in 1794 for these short-stemmed and upward-facing plants, originally thought to be the result of *L. dauricum × L. concolor*. The pollen parent is in fact more likely to have been either natural hybrids or the species *L. maculatum*. These plants were crossed with the European species *L. bulbiferum* var. *croceum* to produce an improved series marketed as *L. × hollandicum* from 1879 onward. (*L. × umbellatum* was a synonym used until only a decade ago.)

Initially the Asiatic hybrids melting pot was derived from species such as *L. lancifolium, L. davidii, L. leitchlinii, L. amabile, L. maculatum, L. dauricum,* and *L. bulbiferum*, as well as early hybrid series such as *L. × maculatum, L. × hollandicum,* and *L. × umbellatum.* Other species later added to the diversity. *L. concolor* and *L. pumilum* helped to produce a number of smaller-flowered dainty kinds of lily, such as 'Viva'. More important was the harnessing of the potential of *L. cernuum*, the species to which we can give the credit for most of the pink coloring among Asiatic cultivars. While the species itself can be a fleeting one in cultivation, its hybrids are as reliable as any.

'Crovidii' was bred from *L. bulbiferum* var. *croceum × L. davidii* var. *willmottiae* in the 1920s by J. E. H. Stooke in Herefordshire, England, the bold type indicating the derivation of the name. It was an upward-facing orange-red flower. The red, much-spotted 'Willcrovidii' was then bred from *L. davidii* var. *willmottiae × 'Crovidii'* around 1928 and was given an Award of Merit in 1932. These plants are of interest as being involved in the same breeder's 'Fire King', an outward-facing lily that is still found in catalogs and remains worth growing.

Working at roughly the same time, Isabella Preston, in Ottawa, brought out a series of clones in 1929 known as the Stenographer Group, the result of mating *L. davidii* var. *willmottiae* with seedlings

'**Enchantment**' (1947) was the trailblazer among modern lilies and after half a century still turns in a dazzling performance. The crowded upward-facing heads of vibrant orange are virtually fluorescent. The success of this lily helped to lay the foundations of the entire cut-flower market.

from *L. dauricum*. They ranged from yellow to orange-red and, like 'Fire King', marked an advance on previous hybrids. From the Boyce Thompson Institute in New York came a series bred from *L. lancifolium* (*tigrinum*) × *L.* × *hollandicum* forms. These were given the unmellifluous name Umbtig Group and had flowers in shades of yellow, orange, and red, all spotted purple. The strength of *L. lancifolium* was lent to the hybrids, but they did not inherit the pendent pose.

In the same field, Cecil Patterson raised a series of hybrids in the 1930s at the University of Saskatchewan, with a view to rearing very hardy lilies that could cope with the harsh weather of the Canadian prairies. His most successful crosses were between *L. davidii* var. *willmottiae* and *L. cernuum*. One of these seedlings, No. 37.538, although unable to produce seed, did have fertile pollen and was used on several parents. A pale-colored seedling, *L. davidii* 'Oriel' × 37.538, gave a number of named lilies, including the orange 'Edith Cecilia', and one of the Stenographer Group, 'Grace Marshall' × 37.538, gave 'Lemon Queen'. Both of these lilies were later used by the de Graaff team.

In the 1930s and 1940s, Jan de Graaff gathered together as many hybrids and species as he could at his Oregon Bulb Farms. The idea was to use the best forms available and raise large numbers of hybrid seedlings so the outstanding ones could be selected, propagated, named, and marketed worldwide. Among the Asiatics, the most successful cross was the combining of the Umbtig Group with the lemon-yellow 'Alice Wilson' clone, selected from the *L.* × *maculatum* kinds and given a First Class Certificate as long ago as 1877. Later on, the 1950s saw the introduction of Jan de Graaff's Mid-Century Group, of which the most successful was the prodigious 'Enchantment'. The scale of the hybridization program paid handsome dividends—God was again on the side of the big battalions.

'Fire King' is early into bloom, with columns of wide flowers in shining rich orange and stems reaching to 4–5 feet high. Named in 1933, it is still widely cataloged and grown.

The Mid-Century lilies were crossed with both *L. lancifolium* and *L. amabile,* and it was this last mating that provided the bright yellow lilies 'Destiny' and 'Prosperity', which were favorite garden kinds for a long time. *L. amabile* was also crossed with the better Preston clones, and these resulted in the selection of a range dubbed the Fiesta Group. Colors ranged from deep cherry-reds to pale yellows, with many pastel shades. They had strong, wiry stems, capable of carrying up to 25 flowers in a pendent pose. The Burgundy Group included more 1959 selections from the Fiesta Group, with very rich wine- or cherry-red hanging flowers of thick texture and with recurving petals. However, the outstanding selections have proved to be the golden-lemon Citronella Group, from 1958, which are still marketed and highly valued as garden lilies.

The Citronella plants have hanging flowers, usually of rich gold with a dash of lemon enlivened by a sprinkling of small black dots. Those with somewhat smaller flowers usually have much-reflexed petals in the Martagon style but larger; it is not unusual to have 30 or more flowers on a good stem. Clones with larger flowers will have fewer blooms but are equally effective, and usually their petals are not quite so tightly curled back. Height varies as well, ranging from 4 feet to 6 feet.

The cultivars 'Edith Cecilia' and 'Lemon Queen' were crossed by the de Graaff team with many of the Mid-Century Group, such as yellow 'Destiny', tangerine 'Harmony', and maroon 'Cinnabar'. The next generation from the resulting seedlings gave the first upright pink and pastel Asiatics. The cross 'Edith Cecilia' × 'Lemon Queen' was one of the most exciting of all, since it produced a cornucopia of wonderful seedlings in all sorts of colors, especially many shades of yellow, orange, red, pink, and pastels down to pure white, as well as bicolors. When these were intercrossed, the results were equally successful. The two generations were collectively known as the Harlequin Group (1950). Some outward-facing and pendent clones were named, including the pollenless, pink 'Corsage', dusky-pink 'Discovery', and pure white 'Buccaneer'.

While yellow lilies such as 'Destiny' and 'Prosperity' had dark spots, the breeders Stone and Payne, working in the United States, set out to breed spotless yellows and managed it with a series having the common house name of Connecticut. Much of the breeding blood came from the yellow *L. lancifolium* var. *flaviflorum,* but other important parents included the unspotted 'Gold Urn' from the *L.* × *maculatum* selection 'Helen Carroll', and the Stenographer Group clone 'Grace Marshall'. The Dutch selection from *L.* × *hollandicum* called 'Waarner's Spotless' was also involved.

the north hybrids

The hybrids bred by Dr. Chris North, working in Scotland in the 1960s and 1970s, are fine garden plants, inheriting the graceful pendent pose of L. lankongense *to make them particularly telling. They grow well in the garden, and a stem or two cut and brought inside can make a charming picture, but their pose precludes them from being commercial cut flowers. They range in color from pale creamy pastel shades to blush-pinks, dark pinks, oranges, and reds, all with generous dotting. They increase well, especially in soil that is rich in humus.*

'Eileen North' 1985 (right)
This is one of Dr. North's hybrids using *L. lankongense* and employing embryo culture to manage germination of the seed. These hybrids are all lovely garden plants characterized by wiry stems, narrow leaves, and well-spaced flower heads of determinedly pendent blooms. Many, like 'Eileen North', are attractively speckled and of engaging pastel shades. This grows to 3–4 feet tall. (*L. lankongense* × 'Edith King' × ['Cardinal' × (*L. lancifolium* var. *flaviflorum* × 'Enchantment'])

'Ariadne' 1976 (left)
Dr. North's 'Ariadne' get its pink coloring from *L. lankongense*, in this case mated with the orange-red 'Maxwill', bred from *L. leichtlinii* var. *maximowiczii* × *L. davidii* var. *willmottiae*. The nodding, recurved flowers are rosy pink with spots. Stems can reach up to 6 feet and have many blooms.

tiger lilies

The compilers of catalogs are keen to help customers select cultivars, and to this end will sometimes categorize groups. A popular ploy is to gather together those kinds showing a distinct affinity to the tiger lily (L. lancifolium) *and market them separately as "tiger lilies." This marketing device is not without merit, as many do have the pendent habit, spotted flowers, and narrow foliage of the species, and most have well-recurved petals. 'Yellow Tiger', for example, has well-spaced, semi-pendent blooms of bright lemon-gold, much freckled, the stems reaching somewhat higher than the two illustrated, at around 32 inches. The Twinkle Group selections tend to have larger flowers that face outward or downward. 'Yellow Twinkle' is somewhat like a large Citronella Group selection.*

'Pink Panther' (left)
This lily has somewhat crowded pyramidal heads with flowers tending to face outward but still a little downward-tilted. The color is a blend of buff and dusky pink, being in parts lightly overlaid with a suggestion of tangerine, the whole considerably spotted. The height is around 24–30 inches.

'White Tiger' 1970 (right)
One of the most pleasing tiger lilies, with neatly spaced heads of pendent or semi-pendent flowers in ivory-white, with perhaps a suggestion of green toward their centers. The well-spaced dark-maroon dots add considerably to the attractiveness of the whole. It grows to 3 feet.

'Brushstroke'
A strong lily with widespread, lightly recurving pointed flowers of white or cream dramatically painted with maroon marks. It looks as if someone has dipped a brush into a pot of dark-maroon pigment and painted lines from the center a third of the way up each petal, with accompanying dots to the sides. Capable of producing stems 4–5 feet tall, carrying many wide-open flowers, it can look most arresting. The heads take on a more ivory or cream shade as they mature.

brushmark lilies
Breeding flowers is always full of surprises, both good and bad, and you never know exactly what is going to appear in the next batch of seedlings to bloom. The discovery of the brushmark lilies is an example of the unlikely happening. At Oregon Bulb Farms, a good form of L. leichtlinii *var.* maximowiczii *'Unicolor' was crossed both ways with a Golden Chalice Group clone, 'Golden Wonder', both parents being unspotted flowers. The seedlings were a look-alike batch of orange, outward-facing flowers with spots. These were then interbred to give another generation. The resulting plants were varied, orange and golden flowers with various poses and differing spotting arrangements, but a single plant had upright flowers of soft tangerine with bold blotches of deep maroon-red on each of the petals, something that had never appeared before.*

Pollen of this individual was posted onto 'Connecticut King', with its rich golden centers. About half the resulting seedlings had the "brushmarks"— some red and others the much darker maroon shades. Selections made and planted out did not show the brushmarks nearly as clearly the next season, but they were interbred and the characteristic became stable. Pollen from the best was used on a variety of kinds, including the white 'Sterling Star' (see page 95). The resulting "brushmark" Asiatics, which look as if they have been overpainted, are quite splendidly classy and confound the traditional, conservative thinking that suggests that one does not "gild the lily."

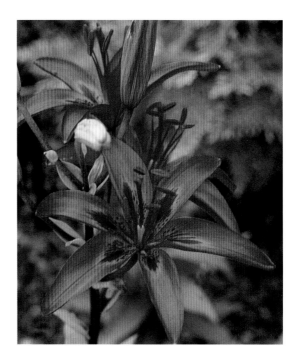

'Red Artiste' 1998
A bright, starry flower of brilliant deep orange-red whose narrow petals are somewhat more orange in the center, where the plum-colored brushmarks are drawn like feathers. This is a sister seedling of 'Cathedral Windows'. Height is 3–5 feet.

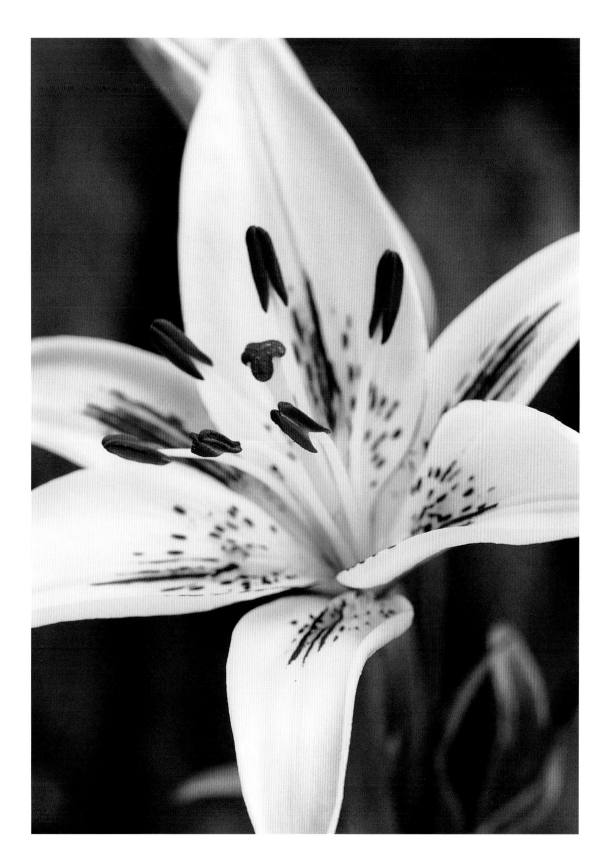

'Flirt'
An engaging lily that certainly catches the eye with its cool looks cosmetically enhanced by beauty spots and dark flashes. 'Flirt' is a sturdy plant that increases readily and blooms from even a small bulb, opening later than many Asiatics. The stems reach about 18 inches high.

dwarf asiatics

Some of the Mid-Century Group were not particularly tall. 'Harmony', with upward-facing, wide-petaled flowers of soft tangerine, would often be content with stems 16–20 inches tall. These were not true dwarfs. By the 1980s a series of dwarfs appeared whose value as pot or patio plants was instantly recognized. They are upward-facing kinds only 10–20 inches high. They can even be shorter—'Denia', for example, is an early blush-pink lily that reaches only about 8 inches, though it has relatively large flowers.

One of the most useful ranges of dwarfs is the Pixie series. These owe much to the influence of 'Red Carpet', a sturdy, upward-facing lily about 12–16 inches tall, first cataloged in 1974. One particular cross of the first-generation seedlings gave a large number of excellent dwarfs that established the Pixies in their strong market position. They are named by color.

'Peach Pixie' 1986
All the Pixies are engaging dwarf plants, coming into floral splendor early in the year. 'Peach Pixie' is no exception; it is a somewhat more subtle color than some, but just as extrovert in demeanor.
(Pastel Group × ['Connecticut Lemonglow' × 'Red Carpet'])

'Golden Joy' (right)
This is a cheerful lily, standing about 16 inches, with glowing large flowers of widely overlapping petals, all in rich golden tones. This is one of the most impressive of the modern introductions, profligate with its gold and a readily increasing bulb.

'Orange Pixie' 1980 (left)
The first Pixie to be introduced and still one of the best. This is a pocket Napoleon—a robust dwarf early engaged in the battle of flowers and the easiest of plants to accommodate in containers or on guard duty at the front of the border. We salute it with its dome of bright blossom. At 10–12 inches it is one of the lower Pixies, but few get higher than 18 inches.
(['Harmony' × 'Sunspot'] × 'Charisma')

color choice among asiatics

Color is usually the first factor governing our choice. All available colors seem popular, but an individual gardener may find certain colors more pleasing or easier to introduce into a garden design.

red/orange

The oranges and reds bring a sense of excitement but may need to be handled with a little care. 'Enchantment' was the trailblazer among modern lilies, with its crowded upward heads of vibrant orange all but fluorescent. Other kinds, such as 'Red Carpet', bloom early and have broader, overlapping petals of uniform deep orange-red, the heads held on sturdy stems. 'Gran Paradiso' stands taller at around 30 inches, its flowers richly colored with pointed petals and some dotting. 'Masa' can be taller still, up to 5 feet, glowing orange-red and a plant of exceptional vigor capable of producing large numbers of stem bulbils.

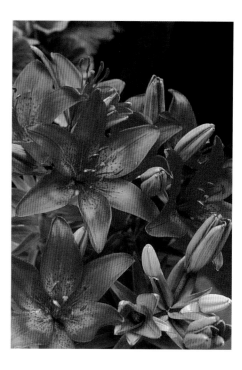

'Victory Joy' (above)
There are many richly colored Asiatics, ranging from red through every subtle variation of orange to gold and yellow. 'Victory Joy' is one of the deeper orange-reds. It is a sturdy plant of fairly modest stature at 18–24 inches, but it is exuberant in bloom, with generous numbers of brilliant, wide flowers staring upward at us.

'Cawlen' (left)
Here is one of the party-going brilliant bicolors, with outward-facing tangerine and gold flowers; the flower stems anchor the display to the ground, but the colors are a vibrant explosive mix, more frequently met with at fireworks displays. This firecracker will light up any border and should be avoided by those of a nervous disposition. It stands 3–4 feet tall.

'Festival' 1980

This tall, elegant lily stands erect with almost black stems, strong dark, narrow foliage and well-spaced flowers. It looks "en fête," but this is not a Mardi Gras extravaganza; all is done in the best possible taste. The mahogany flower buds are dark promises and the opened flowers have true lily grace of line and form, while being an appealing mix of warm pigments, all finished with beauty spots. The petal tips are dark red, the middle sections glowing golden orange but with margins painted deep red, and the centers generously spotted dark chestnut. Standing at least 3 feet high, 'Festival' also has the generosity of nature to hand out quantities of dark bulbils in the leaf axils.

oranges

Plain orange flowers are striking. 'Orange Triumph' was introduced in 1939—not an auspicious time in world history, but this vigorous kind is still with us and makes a strong statement in blazing orange early each season. The 'Apeldoorn' clone currently marketed is a rich orange flower and not the one originally registered in 1965. Its uniform glowing tangerine is effective in upright heads of large, wide-petaled flowers. There has been a succession of flowers of bicolor orange and gold coloring, such as 'Jetfire', bred in 1971.

Quite distinct are flowers such as 'Cathedral Windows' and 'Festival' (see page 87), introduced in 1980; 'Cathedral Windows' is also intricately painted. Its pointed petals are colored rich orange from the tips and for two-thirds of the way down, while the center of the flower is bright as a firework, with each petal having a large flash of gold, which appears to be overlaid by what could be a red feather with even darker lines from the center. The throat is a rich orange. The painted effect of the center is similar to the "brushmark" kinds of lily (page 82).

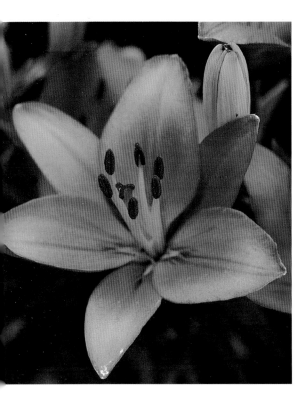

'Orange Triumph' 1939 (below)

This is a "golden oldie," or rather an orange one, that still acts with the enthusiasm of a youngster. This cultivar justifies its place in the most up-to-date collections by virtue of its cheerful, very early blossom. It is often the first of the garden hybrids to bloom without any special encouragement. Its wide, bowl-shaped flowers are the nearest we have among the hybrid brethren to the European species *L. bulbiferum* and its variety *L. bulbiferum* var. *croceum*. The flower form is at odds with modern flowers, with their pointed petals and widely overlapping bases. In 'Orange Triumph' the petals are rounded and the hafts very narrow to allow airspace between the petals and flower centers, an unusual feature. A sturdy plant with shining, broad, neat foliage and plenty of flowers, it stands around 18–24 inches high and increases steadily.

(*L. bulbiferum* var. *croceum* x *L.* x *hollandicum*)

'Castello' 1993 (above)

This is a relative newcomer but has made substantial headway in the crowded field of orange lilies. Its breeding helps as it gains some of its abundant energy from its double chromosome count, being a tetraploid. Its generous heads of boldly posed blooms are wide and vividly orange-red. Strong 3–4-foot stems and clean bright-green foliage complete the picture.

('Napoli' x 'Gran Paradiso')

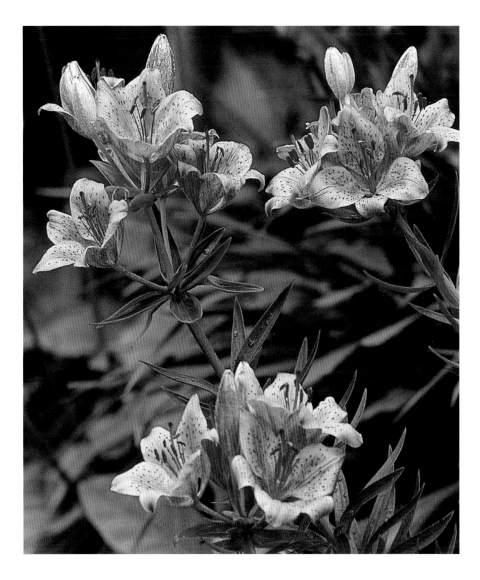

'Jetfire' 1980 (left)

Another gold and orange blend, this lily displays its upward blooms as a wide dome of color over the shining foliage. Standing around 3 feet tall, it can be planted in the border to lighten the early-summer scene or grown in containers and moved to the patio or wherever its bright colors will be appreciated and help lift the spirits.

(*L.* x *hollandicum* x 'Connecticut King')

'Grand Cru' 1991
This sturdy plant was first registered in 1988.
It is a bold, dramatic lily with deep golden
bowls, heavily, even gaudily, overpainted with
mahogany-red in their centers. Its strong
color contrast catches the eye and always
causes comment. It grows to 16 inches. While
it is very popular with many, it is a little too
brash to be one of my top favorites.
(from two seedlings)

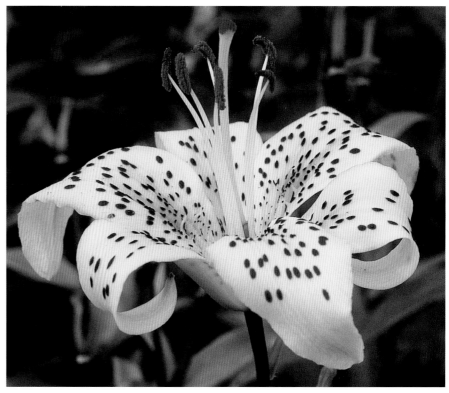

'Tweedledee' 1978
Raised at the Rosewarne experimental
horticultural station in Cornwall, England,
when it was breeding daffodils and lilies. It is
a selection from the Pisky Group, the orange
of this one being overlaid with gold in the
center. The dotting is very much a part of
the overall perky character. 'Tweedledee' is
a sturdy lily at 16 inches high.
(dwarf *L. lancifolium* hybrid × unknown)

yellows

There have been lots of strong yellow cut flowers bred, such as 'Sunray' and the famous 'Connecticut King', which are equally good in the garden, looking healthy with strong stems and shining bright foliage. Many yellow lilies edge toward bicolor status, including 'Luxor', with its darker centers, but others are more dramatically bicolored. 'Yellow Grace' has more pointed petals and bright yellow flowers, with very bold brushmarks so deep maroon as to be almost black, a real eye-catcher. 'Fata Morgana' has proved a popular yellow, perhaps because it is a semi-double kind and a vigorous plant that gives a good account of itself.

'Centro'

A very robust, uniform golden flower gazing upward and making a bold head above stems well-furnished with quite broad, shiny foliage. There are a number of similar cultivars available, some having darker centers, some spotted. Breeders tend to select those seedlings that have broad petals, bold poses, and persistent flowers. It grows to around 3 feet in height.

yellow to cream

The move from yellow to white is marked by some creamy flowers such as the tall 'Roma' and more dwarf 'Medaillon', which is a pale creamy yellow, with each petal having a shaded blotch of pale tangerine; it stands about 2 feet high. 'Doeskin', with semi-pendent flowers, is a peachy cream and champagne blend, with vivid orange anthers. It is a favorite of all those who have tried it.

Yellow Blaze Group 1965 (above) A splendid range of very similar bright yellows that are heavily spotted and have narrow shafted petals, so that one can see air through the centers of the flowers, an increasingly rare sartorial point with modern hybrids, which have wider and wider petals. All are spectacularly freckled. The flowers open at the end of the Asiatic season. The plants are very vigorous and stand around 4–5 feet high. ('Nutmegger' × *L. wilsonii* var. *flavum*)

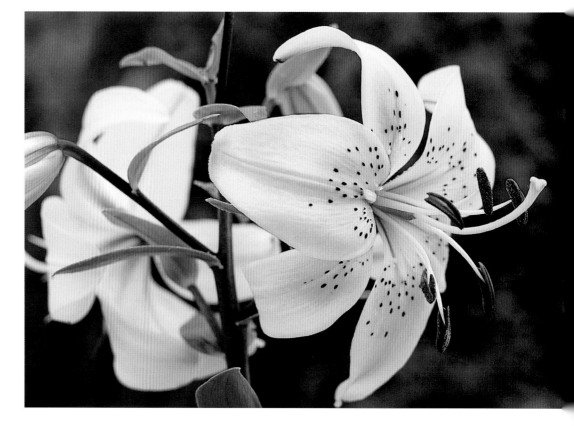

'Hannah North' 1985 (right)
One of the many seedlings of
the North family, this one
displays the characteristic open
pendent pose above wiry
stems. The pastel shades are a
feature of many of these
seedlings. Height 3 feet.
([*L. lankongense* × 'Maxwill'] ×
'Enchantment')

'King Pete' 1977 (left)
This is a regal lily, with its
autocratic outward gaze,
strong stems, and opulent
golden flowers, which are
wide-petaled, pleasingly
enriched toward the center,
and decorated with a few
spots. It grows to 24–30
inches. Long may it reign,
as we are short of these
outward-facing kinds.
(Panamint Group ×
'Connecticut King')

white and cream

The white lilies usually engender a peaceful atmosphere, but there are some with more than a little dash of drama, such as 'Brushstroke' (see page 82). 'Bel Air' is a pure white, the center intricately decorated with many dark purple-mahogany spots. 'Apollo' was a name originally used for a flower akin to L. × testaceum *in 1947 but has since been adopted for a pure white upward-looking Asiatic with broad petals and neat heads on sturdy stems. 'Mont Blanc' (1978) came from the Yellow Blaze Group crossed by a seedling. It has firm-textured, broad-petaled white flowers with pinkish buds and is very lightly spotted.*

'Snow Star' 1985 (above)
One of the best seedlings from 'Sterling Star', this lily is generous with flower and looks good in any garden situation. The flowers are pure white but in some seasons, or in some parts of the world, come with a cream suffusion. It is only lightly dotted and stands at 18 inches. ('Sterling Star' × Asiatic seedling)

'Reinesse' 1989
This is a very effective dwarf lily
with good rich-green foliage as a background to
the broad-domed heads of wide, starry white,
upward-looking flowers. It makes a neat, front-
of-the-border plant or an excellent container
one, rarely standing more than 18 inches high.
('Mont Blanc' × unnamed seedling)

'Sterling Star' 1973 (left)
This was for decades a leading cut flower,
standing 3–4 feet high and having well-
spaced pointed stars with very pale cream
shading and dark central dots. It looks as
elegant in the border as it does in containers.
Though it is taller than many lilies chosen
for pot work, it is a mistake not to use some
tall kinds; this wiry-stemmed cultivar can
look very classy.
(['Lemon Queen' × 'Mega'] × 'Edith Cecilia' ×
'Croesus')

pastel colors

Pastel-colored flowers can be difficult to describe but have a definite appeal. There are a range of colors, forms, and characters. 'Peacock Creation' is a prolific one, with lots of pale peachy stars that fade a little with age. 'Dreamtime', with outward-facing wide blooms, makes well-spaced pyramids of blossoms, all in a soft peachy apricot. This form of display is similar to that of 'Doeskin', but here the color is a buff-champagne enlivened by the brilliant rusty-red anthers. 'Menton' is another outward-facing lily, with strong, wide blooms of creamy peach plus a few maroon spots toward their bases.

Tiger Babies Group 1979
The nodding recurved flowers in shades of peach and pink are heavily dotted and make pyramid heads reaching 3–5 feet. This is one example of the group, which contains similarly colored seedlings in pastel pinks, all enlivened by much spotting. They are fast-increasing bulbs, whose pendent or semi-pendent pose adds to their charm. There is a light perfume, uncommon among Asiatics. ('Pink Tiger' x various Asiatics. 'Pink Tiger' was bred from a *L. lancifolium* hybrid x 'Discovery')

'Eros' 1976
While many Asiatics are of complicated breeding and several generations away from the species with their clearly defined characters, there are some, such as 'Eros', that retain much of the species' individualistic character. This is a wiry-stemmed, free-flowering lily with airy heads of graceful pendent blooms.
([*L. lankongense* × *L. davidii*] × hybrid with blood from 'Redbird', Citronella Group, 'Destiny', and *L. lancifolium* var. *flaviflorum*)

'Corrida' 1998
The blended shades of primrose and pink make this an attractive flower. I find it more pleasing than many flowers with these combined colors, but it needs to be given a good diet, perhaps with an extra dash of potash to strengthen the stems, which can be a bit lax. It grows to 30 inches in height.
(from two seedlings)

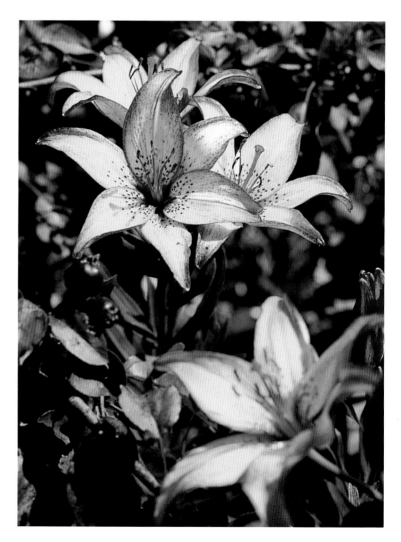

'Silly Girl' 1985 (left)
A popular, cunningly named bicolor in deep pink and pale yellow, it has an engaging freckled character when newly opened, with its colors vividly fresh, but is also attractive when a little faded with age. It has dark buds and stems and neat foliage. It grows to 30 inches tall.
(upward-facing purple Asiatic seedling × 'Prince Charming')

pinks

The introduction of L. cernuum *into breeding brought a fresh color, pink, to the range of lilies. 'Rosita', introduced in 1979, is a good pink lily with dark spots, bred from an Asiatic hybrid crossed with this species. 'Vogue' and 'Vivaldi' are similar, but a little more vigorous. Others vary the pattern by having pink combined with white. 'Zephyr', introduced in 1974, was then one of the richest, purest pinks; it remains a fine kind with pointed petals as richly colored as many of the Orientals. It is sprinkled with a modest number of small dark spots toward the flower centers.*

Now there is a whole range of pinks. Some, like 'Chianti', are a uniform soft baby-pink without spots, while others, such as 'Pink Speckles', have an abundance of them in the inner half of each petal. 'Tinkerbell' and 'Elf' are L. cernuum *seedlings, the first being taller, at 4 feet, and drawn very much to the species' specifications, but it is much more robust than the often fleeting wild plant. The foliage of both is narrow and plentiful.*

'Sorbet' 1988 (left)
A refreshing, perky flower in
pink and white pigments, subtly
arranged and decorated with dots.
In my garden it is grown as a group
below a crab apple tree with purple
foliage, making a very pleasing
pattern of colors. It is a sturdy
plant, growing to 2 feet with bulbs
that increase freely.
('Concorde' × rose-pink seedling)

'Lollipop' 1992
A startling confection with wide
white flowers, each petal tip being
painted a strong pink. The startled
flowers gaze upward, their surprised
look perhaps enforced by the
blushing pink spreading from the
petal tips, the shade an appropriate
"raspberry pink"—the best
lollipops are raspberry flavored.
It grows to 2 feet.

the L A revolution

L. *longiflorum* This is a somewhat tender species that has helped to produce a wide range of completely hardy, very robust LA hybrids when linked with lilies of Asiatic bloodlines.

No, this is not an urban uprising in Los Angeles! LA is the shorthand name for a groundbreaking set of hybrids derived from the mating of the white trumpet Easter lily (*L. longiflorum*, L) with Asiatic hybrids (A). In the normal course of events, such a disparate cross would be unlikely to result in offspring, but various ways of overcoming the inhibitions of the parents have been discovered, and some of these wiles have enabled breeders to open more than one treasure chest.

The *L. longiflorum*–Asiatic partnership had great potential. The Asiatics have their own strong suits, of which hardiness and color range are two. *L. longiflorum* has size and a dynamic growth pattern to contribute. It is one of the fastest-maturing plants, from seed to flower, and responds readily to glasshouse culture. The partnership proved very effective. Any suspicion of tenderness that might have been inherited from the Easter lily was completely overridden by the Asiatic input. The color palette of the hybrids ranges from white and cream to deep golds, oranges, reds, pinks, and some very dark maroons. So far they have been but lightly spotted. The flower form of most LAs has been a broad-petaled, shallow bowl, the dominant poses upward-facing or with slightly tilted blooms.

Bulb growth, either naturally or from scales, is phenomenally rapid. Among my first batch of LA seedlings was an orange-red, which I subsequently named 'Fiery Fred'. The single bulb bloomed for the first time with one strong flower stem. In the fall it was lifted and 13 bulbs found, each of which bloomed the following season. The average number of flowers per stem has been 15.

The LAs have taken the cut-flower market by storm, and they could easily do the same in our gardens. At present, far more than a thousand stems are sold for every bulb purchased in a garden center or through a catalog. But the huge success of the LA mating suggests that there could be other liaisons yet to be tried that will prove just as important in introducing even more diversity.

LILIUM LONGIFLORUM HYBRIDS

L. longiflorum has in recent years been crossed with similar trumpet species to give a number of "improved" forms. 'White Elegance', from *L. longiflorum* seedlings, has long trumpets narrowing to a very restricted base, the pure white very lightly overcast with green or pale primrose toward the base. There are now a number of *L. longiflorum* hybrids that are of trumpet form but colored. 'Casa Rosa' is a midsummer-blooming lily standing 4–5 feet tall and having a good head of trumpet flowers in a rich pink—similar to some of the Pink Perfection Group. A more recent introduction is 'Elegant Lady', which has typical Easter-lily type flowers but with the centers flushed a pleasing dusky pink with a greenish base. It was bred in Holland. Both these plants have the true *L. longiflorum* character and flower pose.

'Fiery Fred' (2003) is strong and free flowering and usually carries more than a dozen large flowers on stout stems but may have more than 30. It has good foliage and freely increasing bulbs. During midsummer it makes a showy statement in the open garden. In pots it will grow to 6 feet, some 18 inches higher than in beds outdoors. It opens early and is in bloom for several weeks.
(*L. longiflorum* × Asiatic seedling)

'Moonshine'
This is a pleasing LA, with smooth, wide, bowl-shaped flowers of cream that fade to white after a few days. It is sturdy and tidy and has good shiny foliage, reaching 3 feet in height.
(*L. longiflorum* × Asiatic seedling)

'Amber Light' 2003
One of the best LAs of this salmon-tangerine coloring, with wide-petaled, large flowers that open relatively early. The darker tones of the center lend emphasis to the overall color and make it glow. Very sturdy stems, usually reaching about 3 feet.
(*L. longiflorum* × Asiatic seedling)

'Rose Madder' 2003
The name describes the rich color of this strong-growing cultivar, which flowers earlier than many LAs. It is not tall, growing to around 30–36 inches, but increases well.
(*L. longiflorum* × Asiatic seedling)

'Rodeo'
One of the first LAs to come onto the market, 'Rodeo' remains one of the dwarfest—but this lack of stature does not inhibit its floral efforts. Plants are hidden below the crowded heads of blooms, which are rich rose-pink with just a hint of lavender and with small orange freckles in the center. To some people, these flowers may seem to be elbowing each other for a place in the sun, but the effect of a group toward the front of the border is delightful. Height 18–24 inches.
(*L. longiflorum* × Asiatic seedling)

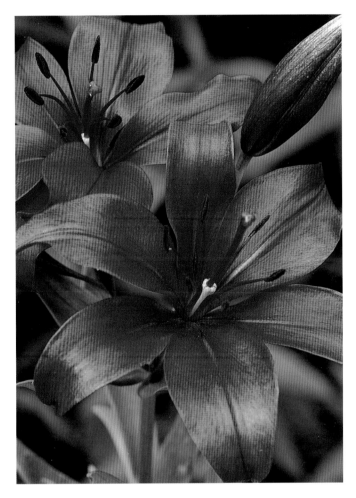

'Showbizz'

The color is similar to that of 'Rodeo', but this cultivar tends to open a little later, and the plants can grow twice as high, with flowers much more widely spaced. The soft rosy-pink blooms shade down to white centers, each flower being rather more trumpet-shaped than the majority of LAs. Height is 3–4 feet.

(*L. longiflorum* × Asiatic seedling)

'Royal Parade'

This is one of the considerable series of LAs introduced with the 'Royal' prefix. A robust plant, with strong stems and shiny dark foliage, its showy wide flowers are well spaced and form bowls of a glowing, deep rose-madder red that holds well. Height is 3 feet.

(*L. longiflorum* × Asiatic seedling)

'Crème de la Crème' 2003
One of my own seedlings and a free-flowering LA with the cream blooms making a wide cover over the plant. The color sometimes has a hint of buff in youth and a few dots to relieve any suggestion of pallid lifelessness. This splendid plant grows to 3–4 feet.
(*L. longiflorum* × Asiatic seedling)

'Aerobic'
One of the best of the cool-colored LAs, this is an ivory shade that fades to near pure white. The shallow bowl form is enhanced by the width of the very smooth petals. This is a good plant, with clean foliage and sturdy stems, flowering in midsummer. Height is about 4 feet.
(*L. longiflorum* × Asiatic seedling)

'Best-seller'

A fast-increasing plant with strong stems and foliage. The uniform pale salmon coloring is held until the flowers fail. Not the most romantic of names—but perhaps it sounds like poetry to Dutch growers. It grows 3.5 feet.

(*L. longiflorum* × Asiatic seedling)

trumpet hybrids

Olympic Group (1946) includes a range of Trumpet hybrids that embraced many colors when first introduced—whites, creams, yellows, and pinks. As the years passed, the whites continued to be marketed as Olympics, while the other colors were segregated or surpassed by individual color strains. Height is 3–6 feet. (bred from *L. sargentiae, L. leucanthum* var. *centifolium, L. brownii,* and *L. sulphureum*)

For many the Trumpets are the quintessential lilies: they have the form, the stateliness, and the perfume. The Trumpet hybrids are certainly an impressive lot. There were a number of valued kinds bred in the first decades of the last century. *L. × sulphurgale* was a range of lilies bred from *L. sulphureum × L. regale*, flowering in 1916 with flowers similar to *L. regale* but opening later. *L. × imperiale* was another early bred kind, the result of crossing *L. regale* with *L. sargentiae*. The original clone of the cross shown in 1920 was similar to the seed parent but with wider and more recurved petals. A selection from this cross, when repeated by Isabella Preston, was called 'George C. Creelman' and for decades it was a valued lily, similar to *L. regale* but with an even darker reverse. Fairly soon, siblings and other similar clones were marketed under this name. These hybrids were used with *L. sulphureum* by Dr. Palmer in Ontario to raise his Sulphur Group in the late 1940s.

The Jan de Graaff team started its work on Trumpets by raising very large numbers of *L. leucanthum* var. *centifolium* and selecting out the best, trying to improve vigor, reinforce the pyramidal structure of the flower head, and select the widest-petaled flowers with the darkest reverses. Having done this, they crossbred the selected plants with *L. sargentiae, L. sulphureum,* and *L. brownii*. From the huge number of seedlings, various color patterns were further selected and interbred. 'Black Dragon' is a strong clone that echoes the qualities of *L. brownii*, with large white trumpets but very dark-purple brown in bud. Each flower of the first stem of 'Black Dragon' was pollinated with a different Trumpet parent. This resulted in

Pink Perfection Group (1950), when first introduced, included plants varying from blush-pink to deep shades. It was the darker ones that appealed to gardeners and so nowadays it is almost exclusively the deep-toned clones, sometimes described as "beet" pink, that are propagated and marketed. This remains one of the standard strains offered some 50 years on. They can be very dramatic plants, with heads capable of a couple of dozen massive flowers. Height varies from 3 feet to 7 feet. (*L. leucanthum × L. sargentiae*)

'Royal Gold' (*L. regale* form, 1955) is usually cataloged as "the golden *Lilium regale*" and first appeared among stock of *L. regale* in the United States in the 1940s. Later, 'Royal Gold' was dignified with single quotation marks, the way a single clone is indicated, but in fact the bulbs now marketed are of two or three look-alike clones. Some are deeper than others with much richer-colored buds—to my mind the more desirable ones. The real origin of 'Royal Gold' is in some doubt. It is possible that some clones are the result of generations of breeding, originally of plants from interbreeding *L. regale* and *L. sulphureum*. The first hybrids were pale yellow only, but with breeding this was concentrated, and the open flowers became deep gold with dark reverses, so the buds were dark. Height is 4–5 feet.

a fine range of white lilies, which, after selection, was the basis of the Black Magic Group, maintained by the controlled crossing of two distinct clones. This should have been the end of the matter as far as nomenclature was concerned, but some plants were vegetatively reproduced and marketed as 'Black Dragon'.

In a similar manner, one clone was selected from the Olympic Group, which were mixed colors—whites, creams, yellows, and pinks—derived from the original mass crossing of Trumpet species. The clone selected, 'Green Dragon', was the best white with a strong chartreuse reverse. If the Olympic Group is found on offer now, the selections are likely to be white Trumpets, with reverses white or lime-green.

One astonishing development in the original Jan de Graaff crossing of Trumpet species was the appearance of flowers with the edges of the petals flushed pink or with pink veining. These were interbred, and quite suddenly there appeared wholly pink flowers, some in pale shades but others quite dark. This was especially surprising as there are inherent factors inhibiting the spread of color through the petals in the species *L. regale, L. brownii,* and *L. leucanthum.* All the pinks were then intensively interbred, resulting in the introduction of the Pink Perfection Group. These are still some of the most popular garden lilies, nowadays represented by the darker clones. They are strong plants, capable of producing large heads of up to 25 flowers on stems that can be 6–7 feet high. In all flowers of this type the depth of color can depend a little on the season and the situation in which the plants grow. Cool weather and light shade help the fullest color to develop. All seedlings showing yellow coloring were similarly interbred (see pages 110–11).

the aurelians

Besides the African Queen Group (1958), an individual clone was introduced as 'African Queen' and this is now the lily that is normally marketed. It is an outstanding, glowing tangerine flower with the three outer-petal reverses a deep reddish brown, to give dark mahogany buds, and the three inner orange petals with a dark brown line down their backs. Both the clone and other members of the group are worthy garden plants. Newly planted bulbs grow to 4 feet but when established may reach 6 feet, carrying 20 or so large blooms per stem.
(selections from Aurelian hybrids—see under Golden Splendor Group)

White Henryi (1945) is an old favorite selected by Leslie Woodruff, a famous lily grower and breeder, over 50 years ago. It is a strong plant standing about 5 feet tall, bearing white flowers with rich, generously painted orange centers, blooming in midsummer. The wide-open, rather flat flowers have their petal tips recurving.
(*L. henryi* × *L. leucanthum* var. *centifolium*)

The potential value of *L. henryi* in breeding was recognized many years ago. The major features of this species that would be useful to incorporate in hybrids make a formidable list: the obvious strength of its bulbs, its longevity, its complete tolerance of alkaline soil, its strong foliage, and its good heads of durable flowers. It may not be the most glamorous of the species, but it has yeoman virtues, and the tangerine coloring is pleasant enough, even if it can fade. The heavy reflexing of the petals might be thought a trifle overdone and the pimpled center something that need not always be greeted with unqualified delight, even when more correctly addressed as papillae.

The first reported success in using this species crossed with a Trumpet was in 1925, when M. E. Debras in France managed to raise one plant from a cross he had made unsuccessfully for a number of years, *L. sargentiae* × *L. henryi*. It was named *L. × aurelianense*. By back-crossing to both parents, he made a start in exploiting the genetic potential. (The original plant favored *L. henryi* in character but became virused and was destroyed.) In the United States a similar cross was made: *L. sulphureum* × *L. henryi*. The result, dating from the mid-1930s, was 'T. A. Havemeyer', a tall, strong plant with wide-open, recurving flowers of buff-orange but with green throats and creamy-yellow petal tips.

The real advance came in 1938, when the de Graaff team grew a thousand bulbs each of *L. henryi* and *L. leucantheum* var. *centifolium* plus substantial numbers of *L. sulphureum* and *L. sargentiae*, together with *L. × aurelianense* and 'T. A. Havemeyer'. *L. henryi* and the hybrids were crossed with the various Trumpet kinds, and the Trumpets were pollinated from the best forms of *L. henryi*. There was a huge harvest of seed, and the resulting seedlings were sorted into various types, known as the Aurelians, the main groups being the Trumpets, the bowl-shaped kinds, and the star-shaped "Sunburst" types. We are still growing plants of these more than 60 years later.

Of the Trumpet-formed hybrids, one of the earliest ranges introduced was the Golden Clarion Group, cataloged in 1948. The strain is still widely grown, normally producing flowers on stems up to 4 feet high. These range from lemon to deep golden, usually with rich chestnut-brown buds, this rich coloring sometimes seeming to permeate the gold. 'Golden Sceptre' is a brilliant rich gold, wide Trumpet with a bronze reverse and the traditional Trumpet perfume.

A number of the richest-colored of the Trumpet-shaped seedlings had flowers with a suffusion or veining of orange, the result of the greater concentration of the pigment carotene. The interbreeding of these gave us the African Queen Group, which is a series of strong-growing plants reaching 5–6 feet and carrying impressive heads of large flowers, dark brown in bud and a glowing apricot-orange when opened.

At the other end of the yellow pigment spectrum was a series of cool lime- and green-yellow flowers. These were marketed as the Golden Dawn Group in 1959. A similar, if not identical, group was the Moonlight Group. It was from the first of these that one clone was selected for intensive propagation and became famous as 'Limelight'. Marketed from 1958 onward, it was a proper Trumpet-shaped flower in cool shades of chartreuse and lime-lemon, standing 3–5 feet tall. It is still available.

The Sunburst Aurelians are flat-faced flowers, perhaps with the petal tips recurving. They were first introduced in 1948, and then new stock was introduced in 1954. The plants are close to *L. henryi* in habit, but not many forms are available nowadays. 'Bright Star', introduced in 1959, is still to be found, a clone that can grow stems 3–5 feet tall, but usually sloping like those of the species. The many flowers are milky white with a honey-orange center and a green nectary star inside.

Golden Splendor Group (1957) is a range of Trumpets with bright golden flowers and buds usually deep maroon but sometimes much less dark. The burgundy stripe on the outside of the petals is more prominent on some than on others. They were selections from the Golden Clarion Group. The flower form is a little more open than most Trumpets, a flared form rather than a narrow, chaste shape. Height ranges from 30 inches to 4 feet. (selections from Golden Clarion Group, which were selections from Aurelian hybrids, bred from *L. aurelianense* × *L. sargentiae* and *L. leucanthum*)

oriental hybrids

'Stargazer' is probably the most important and successful cut flower ever, being upward-facing, heavily perfumed, and durable. It also makes a brilliant container and open-garden lily.

The Oriental species comprise *L. speciosum, L. auratum, L. japonicum, L. rubellum,* and the Trumpets *L. nobilissimum, L. brownii,* and *L. alexandrae.* The large number of Oriental hybrids is almost exclusively the result of the crossing of the first two and the subsequent intercrossing of the hybrids. *L. japonicum* and *L. rubellum* were involved to a much lesser extent. There are now many wonderful Oriental hybrids. Most of those selected for naming are large flowers, most of them beautifully colored. The color range is from pure white through every shade of pink to dark crimson-red, often with gold or yellow pigments used toward the center of the flower or as rays traveling up the middle of the petals. This secondary coloring can be suffused with pink or red but can also be partially merged in or completely independent. All recent yellow cultivars, like 'Golden Stargazer', 'Conca D'Or', and 'Comoro', have been introduced via the cut-flower market.

The first recorded cross between *L. speciosum* and *L. auratum* was made in 1869 by Francis Parkman of Boston, who flowered a lily called 'Parkmanii'. Flowers were described as crimson with white edges, being 12 inches in diameter. 'Jillian Wallace', raised by Roy Wallace in Victoria, Australia, in 1938, was a deep pink with red spots and a white margin. Jan de Graaff used pollen of this on *L. auratum* 'Crimson Queen' to produce 'Empress of India' (1953), a crimson auratum-type with white edges. The same pollen parent was used on *L. auratum* 'Virginale' to give 'Empress of China' (1954), a large white flower with red spots. 'Empress of Japan' (1953) came from *L.* × *parkmanii* × 'Jillian Wallace', this being shining white with a gold band down the center of each petal, plus red spots. These clones, now probably extinct, were used extensively in breeding new hybrids.

In the 1960s the de Graaff team introduced a large range of Orientals bred from (*L. speciosum* × *L. auratum*) × *L. auratum.* These were sorted into named groups, Imperial Crimson Group being deep crimson usually with narrow white margins, Imperial Gold Group being white with a yellow stripe down the center of each petal and much dotted in maroon, and Imperial Silver Group having vivid white flowers usually with a number of tiny red dots. Another group, Imperial Pink Group, came from a slightly different breeding background (*L. auratum* × *L. speciosum*) × (*L. auratum* × *L. japonicum*), a series of large, rosy-pink flowers. All these groups have flowers intermediate in size between the species involved. They are substantially larger than *L. speciosum,* with bigger petals, and these are made more of

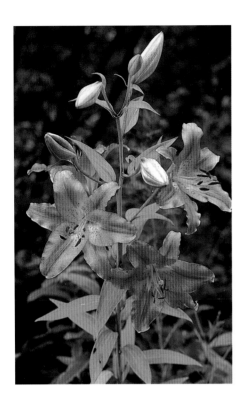

'Le Rêve' (1951) is one of the best-known and most respected cultivars. By the middle of the 1990s there were 116 acres of 'Le Rêve' growing in Holland, a testimony to the esteem in which it is held. The rich, smiling pink tones make it a favorite both as a cut flower and as a garden plant. It has been successfully used in breeding, although its own parents are unknown. It grows to 30–60 inches.

by being spread widely as more or less flat blooms—though the petal tips may recurve a little. The most impressive clones of Imperial Crimson Group can measure 7–8 inches across, the generous number of flowers widely spaced and facing outward on stems 3–5 feet high; they bloom in late summer. Stocks of these Imperials are still available today.

The best known of all the flat-faced Orientals is 'Stargazer', which was first introduced in 1975 of unknown parents. With its upward-facing blooms, it has proved the leading cut-flower lily and may be the most successful cut flower of any type ever. It blooms well off very small bulbs, and these are produced in huge numbers to give stems with around four or five blooms; but in the garden, bulbs can grow larger, with taller stems up to 4ft. (1.2m.) and carrying more blooms. The deep crimson is edged with white, as if ceremonial clothing edged in ermine. Each bloom has the typical Oriental central nectary star of lime green. It is a sturdy lily and can make a fine pot plant.

It was a bold move to call another fine lily 'White Stargazer', as it invites comparison in appearance and performance with its namesake. However, it is deservedly named, as it is also upward-facing and has sturdy, wiry stems of the same height, good dark foliage, and, above all, wide, durable flowers in stunning snowy white with dark anthers and green nectary furrows. 'Casa Nova' is a seedling of 'Casa Blanca' (see page 116), with very large wide flowers of terrific substance that make a big feature of the thread-like papillae and green throat. With upward-facing blooms on stems some 4–5 feet tall, it lives its life in a cloud of perfume. Another impressive white Oriental is 'Phoenix', an outward-facing flower with wide petals and a glistening, snowy purity.

The Orientals are frightened of alkalinity—sensibly, as it kills them. They are therefore often grown in pots by gardeners who have alkaline soils, and they make quite wonderful container plants. I enjoy the tall kinds in pots, but there are dwarf forms that can be excellent on the patio, and these are the easiest of things to grow. I am probably not alone in thinking that maybe some of these could be just a touch incongruous, with their large flowers on short stems, but I try to school myself out of this purist attitude of mind. The trio 'Mr. Ed', 'Mr. Sam', and 'Mr. Ruud' are very short, all about 16 inches high. They have been popular pot plants for a decade or two and appear to be keeping their place. They are outward-facing, each stem holding three or four relatively large blooms. 'Mr. Ed' is nearly all pure white but has a series of tiny red dots and rusty anthers to give some contrast. 'Mr. Ruud' is similarly broad-petaled and a shallow, wide bowl shape, but each petal is boldly painted with a golden ray to look like a miniature *L. auratum*. 'Mr. Sam' is a rich crimson-pink that pales to white at the margins. The bulbs increase steadily and bloom early for an Oriental, in early to midsummer.

'Pink Ribbons' 1972
A gorgeous package in the traditional Oriental style, this is a galaxy of broad stars in many shades of pink contained in a cloud of warm fragrance. Like all the Orientals, it makes a fabulous container plant but is just as happy in the border where the soil is well-worked and free of alkalinity, and will be a star actor in the showier parts of the garden where a theatrical performance is desired. It could look a little out of place or even surrealistic in the more natural surrounds of a wild garden. Midsummer blooming, it grows to about 30 inches in its first season and probably a little taller the following year. The flowers are 6 inches in diameter.

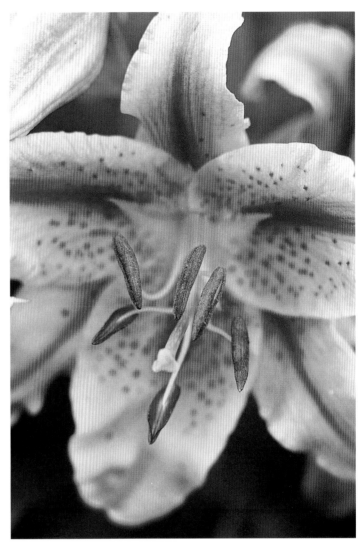

'Spellbound'

A bewitching new Oriental, 'Spellbound' has a bold upward and outward pose, strong stems, and a generous flowering habit, all of which endear it to gardeners, but of course it is the colors that play the major role. The soft gradations of the pinks, the paler golden center, and the sprinkle of dark spots make up a color design that quietly enchants rather than demands attention. Standing 30–36 inches tall, it flowers in midsummer and has the latest in exotic scents.

'Mona Lisa'

A popular Dutch-bred lily growing to about 20 inches, with large blooms tilted upward or outward to display deep, glowing pink, broad-petaled, shallow, bowl-shaped blooms, the deeper pink of the center shading to rosy pink and then to white margins. They are very generously freckled with dark red spots. White margins, greenish throats, and perfume finish the whole. This is a regular catalog listing, grown in large numbers as a pot plant, as it is dwarf, sturdy, with wide, clean foliage, and easy and free with its large flowers. It tends to bloom earlier than many Orientals.

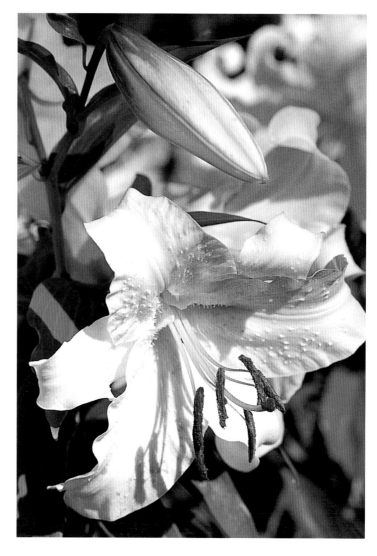

'Siberia'

This is reckoned by many professional growers to be the best upright white Oriental yet in commerce, though the lower blooms of the large head tend to face outward. The flowers are vividly white with a green center and rich rusty anthers. Broad petals have tips somewhat recurved and margins lightly waved. Height to 3 feet.

'Casa Blanca'

A hugely successful introduction of the New Zealand firm Lilies International, which began large-scale breeding in the 1970s, this is an outstanding pure white with massive outward-facing blooms measuring at least 6–8 inches across. Carried on good 3-foot stems in the garden, it will increase its height if grown under glass. It is later in bloom than some Orientals. The dark anthers and a greenish hint to the throat make the flowers even more telling. Displayed with air around each bloom, they look delightful; while officially "flat-faced," the blooms are really shallow bowls with the petal tips recurved. Their pose makes them more difficult to market as a cut flower in comparison to the upright whites, but the flower is so impressive that it is often a first choice for special displays.

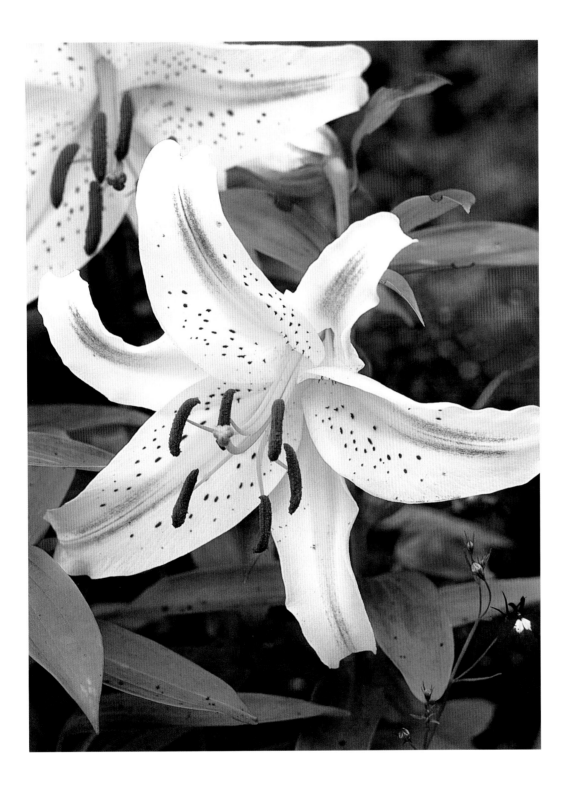

'Arena'

This lily has dazzling outward-facing flowers with widespread petals of white but with golden centers reaching down to the throat, which make it closer to the standard *L. auratum* type than many; the white gives way to crimson-pink toward each petal tip. This richer coloring is also used to fleck the papillae to the side of the golden nectary approaches. Being sturdy and not too tall, this makes an excellent pot plant, with its large, wide flowers looking outward. It is a persistent, hardy lily that increases steadily. It grows to around 30 inches high.

'Star Drift'

This is a wide-open flower of rich crimson-pink with darker rays in the petal centers and with papillae touched with dark red. The margins are clearly defined white areas, giving extra emphasis to the shape of the blooms. The nectary areas form a bright green central star, and the pose is upward and somewhat outward.

'Color Parade'

Although its name is apparently unregistered, this cultivar has been grown for a considerable time and is still worth having. The richly colored flowers are well-formed and long-lasting and are pleasingly shaded a deeper color in the petal centers, fading toward the margins. It grows 30–36 inches tall. It is shown here nearly twice its actual size.

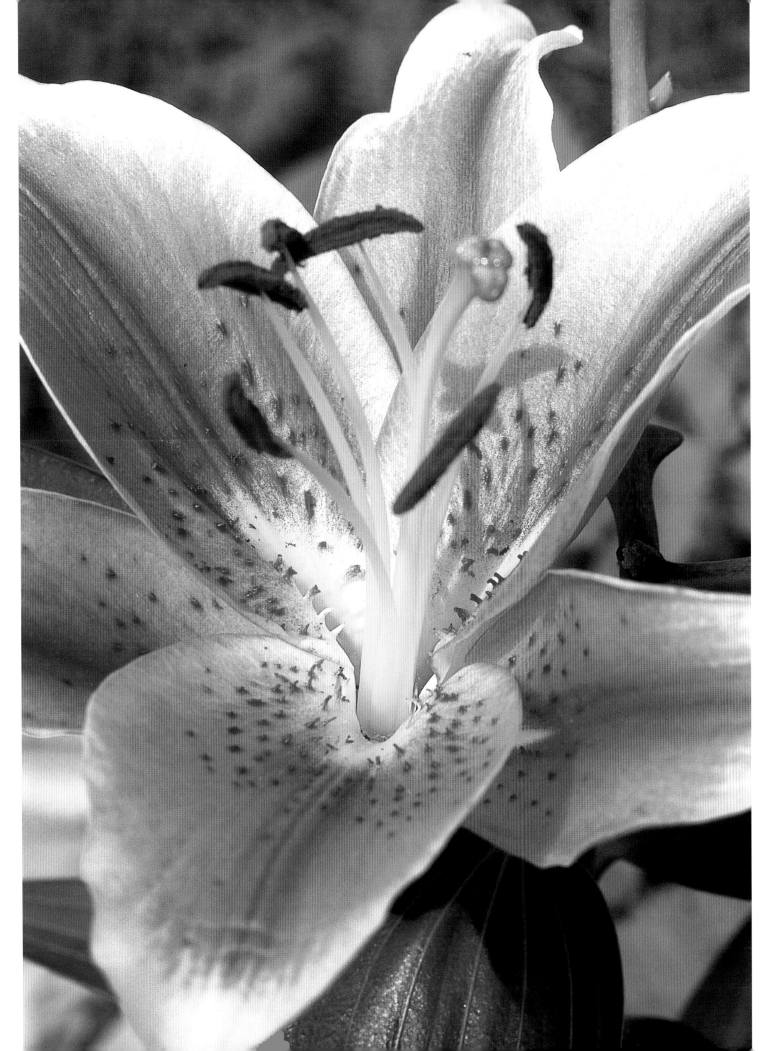

the orienpets

The Achilles heel of the Orientals is their fatal reaction to alkaline soil. Now we have a new race of hybrids that combine the exotic allure of the Orientals with the strength, garden worthiness, and alkalinity tolerance of *L. henryi* and the Trumpet and Aurelian hybrids. These lilies are known among lily fanciers and in catalogs as "Orienpets"—not the most musical of names but one that gives some clue as to their origin, the "pets" being lopped off the word "trumpets." The introduction of this foreign blood has produced plants of outstanding garden worth that are strong, reliable, and improving year after year. They bloom toward the end of the lily season, are at their best in late summer, and can have many large, thick-textured flowers in succession. This breeding phenomenon is one of the biggest advances in the history of lily breeding.

The Orienpets look set to take a leading part in the lily cult, but they are going to do more than this. They will appeal to gardeners with more general interests, as the plants and flowers are very impressive and come into bloom in the second half of summer, when other plants have begun to tire and something fresh and distinctive is especially welcome in the garden.

'Arabesque'
Bred by Peter Schenk in Holland, this is a hugely vigorous plant with massively strong stems 4–6 feet high. It has large, elegant, flat flowers of rich crimson-red, though the petal tips are touched with white and recurve. The petals are impressively wide-spread to make the most of their colors. The blooms face outward in wide heads, a very attractive and effective pose, so that a group of three bulbs can give the impression of far more. The bulbs increase steadily.
('Tetra Black Beauty' × 'Tetra Journey's End')

'Scheherazade' (left)
Always making a big impression, this
has proved one of the most popular
of the Orienpets with gardeners in
the United States and elsewhere. Bred
from the yellow Aurelian 'Thunderbolt'
× 'Tetra Black Beauty', 'Scheherazade'
is a fantastic plant with many pendent
crimson and white flowers, wider than
those of 'Black Beauty' but with tips
recurving. The prominent green
nectary stars are surrounded by the
dominant dark crimson, with only
narrow margins and tips of white.
Bulbs of this fantastic Orienpet
should be sold with ladders. The first
year it may be 3–5 feet tall, but
established plants will be much taller.
We have had stems well over 9 feet
high, each with 40 or more blooms.

'Black Beauty' 1957 (right)
This is an outstanding garden lily,
the first of the Orienpets to take its
place in catalogs and in gardens. It
has very recurved, *L. speciosum*-type
flowers of dark crimson, a "black-
red," which are enlivened by very
narrow white margins. The green
star center is prominent. It stands
some 3–5 feet high with sloping
stems and many semi-pendent
blooms. It is a prodigy of vigor. As
the bulbs establish themselves, the
payload of the stems increases—50
is fairly normal, 100 is perfectly
possible, and 150 is not unknown!
This clone is sterile; but a fertile
one, giving seed and viable pollen,
was artificially produced, a
tetraploid kind marketed as 'Tetra
Black Beauty'. It is similar but of
even firmer texture.
(*L. speciosum* var. *rubrum* × *L. henryi*)

'Silk Road' (left)

Another gutsy Orienpet, this time with trumpet genes showing some influence in the form of the flowers, which are flared, deep bowl-trumpets instead of the "starry" or recurved forms of most others. Perhaps we can also detect trumpet influence in the perfume and in the substantial size of the large, long buds. It is a tall, strong plant that blooms earlier than most of its relatives. The large, heavily perfumed flowers form wide bowls of a rich crimson-pink, becoming darker toward the center but white at the margins and tips. These blooms face outward or tilt slightly downward. Each season sees an increase in the size of the bulb, the height of the 4–6-foot stems, and the number of flowers.

'Catherine the Great' (right)

This is at present the leading yellow Orienpet. Strong 6-foot stems hold spaced heads of large flowers that face outward. The trumpet ancestry can be seen in the stems, foliage, and large bud forms, as well as in the yellow pigments of the flowers. In bud and while opening, they could be taken to be trumpets, but they open widely to form wide bowls of thick-textured, slightly ruffled petals. The flowers are held more or less horizontally and are quite late into bloom. The color is normally a cool primrose, with darker, more golden tones toward the center and base of each petal; the margins can look nearly white in some seasons. The cooler the weather, the deeper are the primrose-gold shades.

The dynamic, exotic-looking lily genus is one of the most exciting features of contemporary horticulture. And while exotic things are attractive, they often suggest difficulty. But any such fears about lilies will be banished by this practical, straightforward guide to planting and cultivation.

growing lilies

Lilies are in many ways the gardener's ideal hobby plant, being one that will respond to the restricted care of a busy person but also one that will reward extra study and can offer a series of challenges. The range of interesting propagation methods will delight many gardeners, and those growers who venture into breeding their own cultivars are likely to prefer this to more staid pursuits.

The hybridization of lilies has successfully overcome any inhibitions that the species might have about cultivation, to such a happy extent that lilies have become one of the easiest garden plants to grow and to propagate. They are certainly the most straightforward and trouble-free bulbs to grow as container plants, being far more amenable than daffodils, tulips, hyacinths, and other bulbs. Before planting your lilies, it is as well to understand their life cycle, or how they will behave throughout the year.

growing lilies: planting

Lilies enjoy well-drained and cultivated soils that are neutral or slightly acid. The addition of rotted organic matter will improve soil fertility and help maintain an open, fibrous mix.

CYCLE OF GROWTH

Bulbs planted in early fall or early spring get into action quickly, with roots emerging from the basal plate of the bulb and, in the spring, a stem rising toward the soil surface. In the majority of lilies this stem gives rise to its own system of roots, usually in rings that are pressing outward even as the stem reaches for the surface. The stem produces its quota of leaves, sometimes a huge number, but in some kinds only a sparse scattering. Flowers may number from a singleton to over 150 per stem! After the flowers have faded, seed pods may develop. These will split vertically to allow the flat disk-like seeds to float away from each of the three chambers, each chamber having two piles of seeds. By now, the plant has begun to wind down for the winter "dormant" months, and leaves and stem turn pale brown.

The end of summer will be the time to lift early flowering lilies if they are due to be split up and given more room. Later-flowering kinds can be lifted some weeks before the onset of winter weather. The idea is to replant immediately in pots or in the open and allow the bulbs to begin to form a new rooting system before the onset of cold, wet weather. Frosty conditions combined with wet weather can be particularly bad for lilies in pots because the frost can penetrate not only from the top but also from the sides, so aim to keep the plants on the dry side through the winter.

buying lily bulbs

A selection of lily bulbs may be offered for sale loose in a garden center. Always pick the plumpest with a minimum of bruising, and avoid those with withered scales.

For gardeners the most obvious sources of bulbs are garden centers or mail-order catalogs. Garden centers may have a dozen or a couple of dozen lilies, whereas a good general bulb catalog may list as many as 70 kinds and a lily specialist could produce a catalog with well over a hundred different cultivars and species. The prices of bulbs vary; a few of the rarer or newer types can be very expensive, but generally the lower price per bulb reflects the relative ease with which bulbs can be increased. You can order from bulb traders with considerable confidence, since they need repeat orders to keep their business healthy and will therefore be careful about the bulbs they supply. The bulbs should be true to name, healthy, and packed carefully to prevent bruising or other damage during transit. Some of these suppliers are listed under Further Information (on page 156).

The selection offered by large garden centers, although not as wide as that of specialist firms, can still be impressive and customers have the benefit of being able to see the bulbs they are purchasing. The smaller number of kinds offered may mean that only the most reliable garden plants are included. Old favorites are not ignored, but surprisingly, new lilies are often introduced at garden centers before they get into the bulb suppliers' catalogs. Garden centers now also provide a wide choice of potted lilies, usually three to a pot, displayed with green flower buds not far from coloring and thus only a few weeks before flowering. These are usually a good value, often costing little more than the price of three individual bulbs. Favorite kinds for this enterprise are the dwarf lilies, including several Asiatic series, such as the variously colored Pixies, reaching heights of 10–15 inches. Low-growing Orientals such as 'Mona Lisa' are also sold in this way.

CHOOSING BULBS

The best time to plant lilies is in early fall or early spring (see Planting, page 130), and you can buy your bulbs at these times. If you are buying by mail order, it's best to order early, to avoid the risk of missing kinds that may sell out and to allow the supplier to send your bulbs at an appropriate time. If bulbs are bought or received in the middle of winter, when planting conditions are next to impossible, plant them up in pots, and keep these under cool cover until early spring, when the whole potful can be planted out.

If buying bulbs at a garden center, you will be able to choose the ones you feel are the best. Always look for plump, undamaged bulbs; all other things being equal, a good big one beats a good little one. Because lily bulbs are without any protective layers, they are easily bruised. Bruising can start rotting, and any brown rotting around the base is a real danger sign. Blue penicillin mold may appear on slightly damaged tissue, but this need not be too great a cause for concern, since the small area affected can be cut away with a sharp knife and the exposed tissue dusted or soaked with fungicide before planting. Avoid bulbs with stems growing from them and trying to force their way out of the packet. This does not mean that you should avoid any bulb with the beginning of growth in the nose, as such bulbs will generally grow well if planted immediately.

The usual format is to offer bulbs singly, or in twos or threes, in plastic packets with color illustrations. Most good garden centers house packaged bulbs in reasonable conditions and will remove them from sale if they deteriorate. Bulbs that appear flaccid may be restored to better condition if covered for a day or two with moist peat or similar material. However, it is not unusual to find packets that have been hanging around for ages in which the bulbs are completely dehydrated; there will be no resurrecting these—they are as dead as the well-known doornail. Packaged bulbs are likely to be of a reasonable rather than fully mature size. Considerations of packaging, transportation, weight, and general ease of handling make it nearly prohibitive to use the size of bulbs that you will grow from the

Packets should give the name of the lily, usually its type (Trumpet, Asiatic, or Oriental), its height, and basic suggestions about its culture.

ones you buy. But at the end of their first season you should be able to see a most satisfying increase in size.

Other bulbs may be displayed loose, perhaps with some peat around them to minimize bruising and keep them from drying out too much. These loose bulbs are often larger and, if bought fresh, will give excellent results; they should be more prolific of bloom than the smaller packaged bulbs of the same cultivar. There are good reasons for purchasing these bulbs soon after they are put on display. You will be picking out the best bulbs. The juicier they are, the more quickly they will respond by growing strongly. And although some kinds of lily have bulbs that look distinctly different from others, all the Trumpet kinds, for example, look alike. Previous browsers may have returned bulbs to the wrong compartment so that some months later there is a chance of your finding a variety you didn't choose.

We live in a consumer age of special offers, and these appear in the gardening world as elsewhere. Sometimes they are a good value, but I would not usually recommend buying the mixed packets of lilies, as they are unnamed and will all have different specifications. If you are not worried about knowing the names and think a small gamble worth trying, you could plant out a packet of these, and then if any particularly take your fancy, those bulbs can be propagated for following seasons.

planting in beds and borders

Bulbs can be planted outside in fall or spring. In years past, the usual advice was to plant early in the fall to allow the bulbs to get well rooted before winter. This remains a sensible procedure, but the advice dates from a time when bulbs were not readily available in spring and the technology to store bulbs for long periods without any deterioration was unavailable or not exploited. In heavy soils, autumn-planted bulbs may have to deal with wet conditions for some months, and such soils may have a population of slugs that could attack the bulbs. If you plant bulbs in the fall, it is wise to do it early, to allow the rooting system to be well formed and the soil structure to settle before the winter. The resulting plants can grow taller than spring-planted ones.

Early spring has the advantage of a soil that is beginning to warm up and stimulate the growth of all plants. The lily bulbs are likely to produce roots rapidly and not be long forcing their shoots upward. A few slug pellets can be laid on the soil or other precautions taken to minimize the likelihood of damage. Once the lilies have broken through the soil, growth becomes increasingly slug-resistant. It may also perhaps be a little easier in spring to see how the lilies could play their part in the overall garden plan.

Planting sites should be well dug and weed-free; where necessary, organic matter and grit should be added. The aim is to provide an open-structured soil rich in humus, after which drainage should be adequate. Check the health of your bulbs before proceeding to plant (see page 128).

SITES AND SOILS

As we have seen, lilies will grow in most garden soils without too much trouble. A very alkaline soil will preclude some lilies and will require the addition of rotted organic matter to keep even the alkaline-tolerant kinds really happy. Heavy clays are not ideal, as they can compact and leave drainage poor, with little air in the soil. The perfect soil would be a healthy loam, slightly on the acid side of neutral, with a good ration of organic material incorporated to keep the whole mix open and fibrous.

Humus or compost is a vital ingredient in a healthy garden soil. It is the complex chemical result of the decomposition of living matter, an organic residue. It helps provide an open structure and so aids drainage, but it is also water-retentive and helps keep plants going in times of water shortage. It has an important role in soil fertility. The best source of humus is well-rotted organic matter such as garden compost or rotted horse manure.

Lily bulbs and roots will be happiest in soil that is shaded, with the exception of *L. candidum,* which seems to welcome sun on its soil. And while lilies appear to grow best when associated with other plants, they do not like being crowded or too

L. speciosum, seen here with deep red dahlias, is one of the last lilies to bloom and brings a freshness to the autumn garden scene.

heavily shaded. The maxim is "Toes in the shade, faces in the sun." The growing plants enjoy an airy environment; still, humid conditions can foster fungus diseases such as botrytis. On the other hand, no lily is going to be very pleased to find itself living in a wind tunnel or in any position subject to strong gales.

pH values

The acidity or alkalinity of a soil is measured on a scale of 1 to 14, with 7 being neutral. Higher numbers point to increasing alkalinity, lower ones to greater acidity. There is a range of simple testing kits that will help you determine the pH level of your soil, and it is worth taking several readings from different areas of the garden, as levels can fluctuate considerably within a relatively short distance. For instance, against an old wall using old-fashioned mortar containing lime there will have been a gradual addition of soluble lime salts from the rain passing over the wall. Readings from 5.5 to 7.5 may be taken as ideal.

Good sense should dictate that gardeners grow the plants that suit their soils, but most gardeners still want to try acid-loving plants when their soil is alkaline, and vice versa. Of course soils can be doctored by the addition of lime to increase alkalinity or chemicals that will encourage acidity. The addition of humus, in the form of well-rotted organic matter, will help swing the level to the acid side, but it will take a lot to move the reading a complete point; any alkalinity present will break down the humus. Fortunately, most gardens have soils that are neutral or within a short measure of this on either side of the scale, and such soils will be fine for most lilies.

Drainage

The most important feature of lily soils is their drainage. The roots of the bulbs love to get delving into an open-structured soil with a lot of air in it. Grit and humus will help to enhance such a structure. There may be areas of the garden that are poorly drained, and here it will pay dividends to make drains to take away standing or surplus water. Such drains can be made by half-filling trenches with rubble covered with a semi-impervious layer of material that will prevent it from immediately filling with soil. Turf, tree, or shrub "brushwood" or even newspapers will serve as this layer. The slope away to lower ground or to more important drains need not be dramatic, but it needs to be there.

Lilies will enjoy fairly plentiful moisture during their active growing months, but through the winter they will be happier to be kept drier. Standing water with long-sodden soil will adversely affect the bulbs, since lilies dislike stagnant conditions, and this especially applies in the winter. Rotting can start and fungus diseases be encouraged by continuously wet soil. You might give some of the fussy species some protection from excessive winter wet in the form of cloches or sheets of glass over their sites, but this should not be needed by most lilies or in most sites. In northern climates the bulbs may likely be covered by a blanket of snow, which keeps them from being too wet for several months. The bulbs will not relish being frozen, but moderate cold is clearly not something to which they object.

PLANTING DEPTH AND DISTANCE

The depth at which you plant the bulbs and the distance apart will vary according to the type of lily.

ASIATIC LILIES will be best with at least 4 inches of soil over the top of the bulbs, or planted slightly deeper in very light soil. If you intend to lift the bulbs after a season, you can plant them as close as 6 inches apart, but if they are to be left for two or three years, allow 12 inches for the increasing number of bulbs.

SPECIES LILIES WITH SMALL BULBS, such as *L. concolor* and *L. pumilum*, can be planted less deeply, with 3 inches of soil covering them, and as close as 4–6 inches.

LILIUM CANDIDUM has quite large, rather loose-scaled bulbs and these are treated differently from all other kinds. Plant the bulbs with their noses close to the soil surface, as they may struggle if planted deeply, and 8–10 inches apart.

TRUMPET LILIES with large bulbs, such as *L. regale* and hybrids like Pink Perfection Group, need to be planted more deeply, at 6–8 inches, as do such strong-growing lilies as the Orienpets 'Black Beauty' and the tall 'Scheherazade'. Their large flowering heads mean that they also need plenty of room: 15 inches apart would be a minimum when planting for a stay of two or more years. I usually plant 'Scheherazade' with at least 24 inches between the bulbs, sometimes more.

1 Lay the bulbs on well-prepared soil in their rough spacings, and make individual holes using a trowel.

2 The hole's depth will depend on the type of bulb (see opposite); most need at least 4 inches of soil over them.

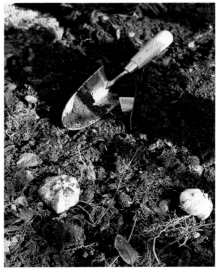

3 Place the bulb in its hole with the roots carefully spread out, and cover with soil.

4 Level the soil and label the bulb to indicate its position, then plant others in the group.

THE RHIZOMATOUS BULBS of *L. pardalinum* and its hybrids are best planted 4 inches deep. As these are likely to remain *in situ* for a few seasons, it would be a mistake to plant too closely—consider 12 inches apart a minimum. The behavior of these bulbs can be unusual: as they grow and spread sideways, they appear to travel some distance toward the surface. They must find the depth at which they are happiest, but it is best to start freshly introduced bulbs with a 4-inch cover of soil. This keeps them cool and moist as they establish themselves.

planting in pots and containers

Lilies almost always do well in containers, and gardeners new to growing lilies will often try them first in this way. Having grown bulbs of many types for well over 50 years, I am convinced that lilies are by far the easiest of any bulb to grow in pots and other containers. Potted bulbs are versatile: they can be given individual care and placed in a position to overwinter safely, or they can be given some warmth under glass to encourage earlier blooming. Generally speaking, the bigger the pot, the easier it is to grow good plants. A reasonably large amount of potting mix can be kept moist and at an even temperature much more easily than the quantity in a small pot. Pots are measured both by their diameter and by their capacity, but the amount they can hold is perhaps the more relevant measurement. I like to use earthenware pots, where they are going to be seen, but use plastic ones just as readily. Plastic pots delay the drying out of the potting mixture a little longer.

Apart from the considerations of space for the bulbs and the food supply from the soil mixture, the pot size can be important for the stability of the whole, once the plants have grown. Three tall lilies, perhaps Trumpet kinds, can easily reach 4–6 feet if planted early or grown for a second year in a pot. This tall growth can catch the wind, and the container may be blown over if it is not securely weighed down. A large pot may not be completely stable, but it will be less vulnerable than a smaller one.

POT SIZES

- A pot about 7 inches in diameter would be the smallest practical size; this could serve for one normal Asiatic or three dwarf Asiatics. But the small size means that once the plants grow there can be problems preventing the soil mixture from drying out, and in a crowded pot it is difficult to manage proper watering from above.

- A pot 7.5 inches in diameter is the minimum size for a single bulb of a Trumpet or similar-sized lily and a reasonable size for three normal Asiatics— but this size may still be too small for many other kinds of lily.

- A pot 9 inches in diameter is good for three Asiatics or Orientals. It could house one large or three small Trumpets.

- A pot 10 inches in diameter is considered a minimum size for three Trumpets or three large Orientals.

Half-barrels and other similarly generous containers are ideal for lilies, provided they have adequate drainage holes. They were much favored in the past, when it

Oriental lilies, such as 'Arena', make a splendid display in a container, serving as a focal point against a background of feathery foliage.

was *de rigueur* to have crowded tubs of *L. regale* in any important garden. Nowadays we have a much wider choice of lilies to grow in such containers, though the regal lily could still be many gardeners' first choice. Half-barrels have the advantage of being large enough to host a number of plants, creating a mini garden that can look colorful for months with and without lilies. Ideally such tubs or other large containers should be raised up a little way off the ground, whether it is on soil, gravel, or paving. This will aid drainage, help prevent the incursion of slugs and snails, and lessen the chances of the container base rotting or deteriorating.

DISPLAYING LILIES IN POTS

A single lily in a pot can look splendid, but it cannot compare to the display of a trio growing together. Whenever possible, plant three bulbs per pot, and always of the same cultivar; try also to have matching-sized bulbs so that the performance of all will be equal. Really large pots may be able to take more than three bulbs and give an even more sumptuous effect.

Most standard Asiatics grow to about 32 inches tall, and these will do well in pots without being too vulnerable to wind. Even taller kinds, such as those of the Pink Perfection Group and other tall Trumpets, can be excellent in containers, too, though it may be wise to add some supporting canes or twigs at the same time as potting the bulbs. Then, as the plants grow taller, it will be prudent to make sure the pot is well anchored. The bulbs will probably grow quite a lot taller if left in the same pot for a second year, especially if you scrape away the top layer of potting mix at the end of the first growing season and replace it with fresh material.

POTTING MIXTURES

Most Asiatics and Trumpets will cope with potting mixtures that contain a little lime; therefore, it is permissible to use a loam- or soil-based potting mixture, with only a little fertilizer. The advantages of the loam-based mixtures over peat/humus-based ("general purpose") mixtures are that they drain more freely, have more air in their structure, and are easier to water if dryish. Humus-based mixtures can also be good, especially with plenty of grit added.

Potting mixtures with a pH of between 6.3 and 7.0 can safely be used for

PLANTING LILIES IN CONTAINERS

1 Cover the drainage hole with a layer of broken crocks or pieces of polystyrene to prevent soil from draining away.

2 Using a trowel, cover the bottom of the container with an appropriate potting mixture, then place the bulbs on top.

Oriental lilies. The addition of grit may make these mixtures easier to water—something that can be difficult if the mixture is allowed to dry out. Dried-out pots are best lowered into a large vessel filled with water, so that the water can then gradually work its way up through the potting mixture by means of osmosis.

I do not think garden centers have yet started to offer potting mixtures specifically for lilies, though this could happen. Meanwhile, lily fanciers have independently formulated mixtures that seems to suit most lilies. Although a soil-less commercial potting mix may be too free-draining and fast-drying to be completely practical, the addition of extra rotted organic matter helps it retain moisture, slightly acidifies the mix, and makes it a little more root-friendly. I use a mix of equal parts of soil-less commercial potting mix and organic matter; other growers use a similar mix.

In some instances excessive exploitation of natural peat reserves can be detrimental to the environment. Now, however, more and more alternative sources of humus are being made available. Making your own leaf mold by rotting down oak and beech tree leaves is another possible source. And properly made, well-matured material from the compost pile will be like manna from heaven to lilies.

3 Lay the bulbs on top of the potting mix, equally spaced and with their roots carefully spread out.

4 Cover the bulbs with more potting mix so they have a layer of at least 4 inch over their noses (see page 132).

5 Leave a gap of at least 1 inches at the top of the container. Water using a fine rose on a watering can, or soak the soil mix by standing the pot in water.

POT PLANTING ROUTINE

Bulbs can be potted up at any time from the end of summer until late spring. Normally those planted early will do best, but the lily is a resilient pot plant and will respond to a little care if planted late. Pot-grown bulbs are best kept in a cool frost-free spot through the winter, preferably under cover if the weather is wet. The pots of growing lilies may be housed in an unheated greenhouse or cold frame but should be just as happy in the open if it is dry, as they enjoy a buoyant, airy atmosphere. A humid, close atmosphere may encourage fungus diseases such as botrytis. Keep aphids and other pests under control with an occasional spray.

Unless you wish to harvest the seed, cut off the flower heads after blooming without removing any leaves. Continue to water the pots for six weeks or more to keep the bulbs healthy. Toward the end of summer, or in fall, turn out the pots to reclaim the bulbs, together with any increase in the form of divisions of the bulb or bulbils clustering on the subterranean part of the stem. The foliage and stems of earlier-flowering lilies will have lost their vitality and may be turning brown, so they can be twisted away from the bulbs. Replant the bulbs, and perhaps grow the small ones on separately in pots or in the open ground. Make sure that they are all clearly labeled.

pests and diseases

Lily beetles measure about ⅓-inch long and almost half as wide. These pests are very visible, with their flat backs a brilliant orange-red.

The larvae are about the same length when fully grown but are hidden under a revolting mass of excreta. Under this dirty gray mass the creamy grubs steadily eat through the foliage.

PESTS

Lily bulbs are edible, as are the growing plants, and threats from larger pests come from rodents, rabbits, and deer. Fences may have to be put in place to keep out deer and rabbits, which devour the emerging stems with relish. Our present garden was overrun with rabbits when we arrived, so I erected a wire-mesh fence just over 3 feet above ground and more than 12 inches below, with a short length at the base turned at right angles from the garden to deter excavating rabbits. Mice, voles, and rats will find the bulbs a useful source of food, particularly in the winter, and for them cats and humane traps are recommended. The smaller pests affecting lilies include slugs, aphids, vine weevils, and lily beetles.

Lily beetle In Europe, the handsome lily beetle (*Lilioceris lilii*) is the most annoying of the small pests, and in recent years it has appeared in parts of eastern North America. These beetles usually appear in spring and can be active until fall. While the adult beetle is conspicuous, the larvae hide under a mass of excreta that could well be blamed on passing birds. As both the adult beetles and the larvae live off the leaves of lilies, the result of a severe attack can be plants reduced to pathetic stems with a few threads where the foliage has gone.

Because their presence is visible and their identification easily made, the beetle and its larvae can be collected by hand and destroyed. There is one hazard: often their reaction is to fall to the ground, where they turn and lie on their backs, the bright red being replaced by black which makes them almost impossible to see. It is best to lay a sheet of paper under the leaf being attacked before trying to pick off the beetle, so that the falling beast is captured. The second method of attack is to spray the foliage with a systemic insecticide, using a handheld sprayer or a ready-made pressurized can. The beetle and larvae eat their leaf and ingest some of the poison, which usually kills the larvae quickly. The beetle may be a little more resistant, but it moves more sluggishly and can easily be gathered up.

A regular inspection of the plants will ensure that any invasion is spotted early enough to be dealt with. It is only if the pests are left undisturbed that plants are severely attacked. In my experience the most active season for the beetles is in late spring, the time that coincides with the maximum growth rate of the plants and before their flowers start opening.

Lesser pests Slugs and snails can attack lily bulbs and the young stems. They are usually at their most active in early spring, at a time when lily shoots can be emerging from the bulb and breaking the soil surface. A stem can be weakened by nibbling slugs and the whole plant jeopardized. Clean cultivation of the soil will help reduce the slug population, traditional traps can take a useful toll, and pellets

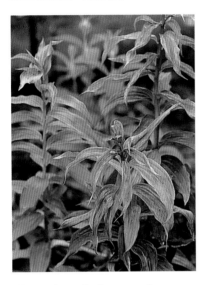

The pale striations on the foliage indicate that this lily is suffering from cucumber mosaic virus. If the plant is not destroyed, the virus can be passed to other healthy plants—most efficiently by aphids.

strategically positioned will deal with others. It is now possible to purchase pellets that are harmless to pets and birds; the dead slugs collected by birds are harmless.

Aphids may attack the growing lily plant, especially the clustered flower buds. These will be killed by systemic or other insecticides. It is best to attack in good time before they have started to damage the tissue of the flowers and cause them to open distorted. The other reason to keep on top of aphids is that as they suck juice from the lilies they may transmit virus they have picked up from infected plants elsewhere. The injection of these viruses will not be immediately evident, but the following year could result in a lot of plants having to be destroyed.

Vine weevils can be a nuisance. The adult is a gray-black insect with brown flecks, about ⅜–inch long, recognized by ridged lines running longitudinally. It feeds on foliage. The plump, creamy-white grubs are more dangerous, as they feed on roots and can leave a plant without the means to support itself. An apparently healthy plant may suddenly wilt, and when the roots are examined, grubs will be found. The vine weevil is not normally a major threat to lilies, but grubs can attack potted bulbs. There are a number of effective chemical treatments.

DISEASES

Virus Of a number of viruses that can attack lilies, by far the most common is the cucumber mosaic virus, which, despite its name, is found in a wide range of plants. The symptoms are pale patterns of stripes on the foliage. When well established, this virus may cause distortion of leaves and flowers and a brittle texture to both. Tulip breaking virus causes a mottled effect on the foliage. Lily symptomless virus is an unusual one that may be suspected when for no reason a plant or group of lilies appears to lose its vitality and look debilitated. This is not widespread at present, so check other possible causes for deterioration of plants before destroying them.

There is no cure for virus, so all attacked bulbs should be destroyed before insects spread it further. It is possible to pass on the trouble if a knife used for cutting an infected stem is then used on a clean plant.

Fungus The widespread *Botrytis elliptica* can cause severe damage when conditions are favorable. It spreads quickly in wet, airless conditions, so humid weather will foster this disease. If lilies are crowded together in places where air movement is restricted, the fungus can attack. It will usually start by turning lower leaves brown, which at first may look like blotches caused by frost. The leaves become limp and wither, and a major attack could leave a whole stem defoliated. Though this looks unsightly and plants are indeed weakened, they are rarely completely killed. Keep the disease at bay by providing plenty of air around your lilies. Spraying with Bordeaux mixture early in the growing season can help control botrytis, but it is not a cure.

For many people, propagation is the heart of gardening, and for them the lily is the ideal hobby plant. It has many successful means of increase. Seed is obviously nature's first choice, and in the wild this is how lilies maintain their presence. Gardeners may follow suit or decide to exploit the plant's natural bulb division in some way—something that is likely to happen more freely under the benign conditions of cultivation than in the wild. Bulblets form on the underground part of the stem of many kinds of lily, while bulbils may appear in the leaf axils of

growing lilies: propagating

some. But the most popular method is to use the ability of scales broken from the bulb to form small bulbs along their fractured edges.

There is a fundamental difference between seed raising and all other methods of propagation, which are vegetative, and both types have advantages. The advantages of vegetative propagation are considerable. First, all new plants will have identical genetic material to the parent bulbs and, being parts of a single clone, will be able to produce a uniform performance. (The definition of "clone" is plants with identical DNA, so separate plants of a clone are effectively divided parts of one individual.) Flowers will be the same, as will blooming time, plant height, and habit. Vegetative propagation is normally also much easier than by seed, as it takes less care than the successful germination and growing on of small seedlings.

Self-pollinated seed from species will broadly reproduce the characteristics of the parents, but there will be some variation, perhaps small but possibly significant. A little change in flower color is easily noticed; very often orange species also have yellow forms due to a lesser concentration of the color pigment carotene. Less obvious may be a tendency to bloom a little later or earlier than the norm. Optimum height of the plants is another variable that can be ascertained only after a period of time. It is always worth renewing stock of species by seed, not only to take advantage of a possible beneficial variation but more importantly to introduce new stock that is free from virus and other diseases.

Virus can be insidious in the way it reduces the overall efficiency of plants. Sometimes this is a rapid process with obvious symptoms; other times the attack may affect the lilies' vitality only slowly, with initially very faint signs. The most worrying factor is that while the effect of virus will be minimal on one lily, if aphids transfer the virus to others the result of infection on the new host can be catastrophic. There is no cure for virus within the usual abilities of an amateur grower, which means that any infected plant reproduced vegetatively will pass the virus to all propagated plants. Obviously the choice of healthy bulbs for propagation is vital.

natural bulb division

Dig at some distance from a stem, as it may not have grown directly upright from the bulb.

The concentric bulb has two noses and is ready to divide, while a new small bulb has been easily detached.

There is huge diversity in the bulbs' natural rates of increase, varying from slowly dividing ones to others with rabbit-like fecundity. Increased rates will depend on the type of bulb, but also on soil and environmental factors. The concentric bulbs of Asiatic hybrids normally split regularly, a reasonably sized bulb easily dividing after a season's growth into two or three bulbs of similar size to the original when planted. LA hybrids can considerably outstrip this performance. Trumpets and Aurelians tend to expand their bulb size before dividing but often develop new, smaller bulbs as side shoots around the base of the bulb or within the outer ring of scales.

After a bulb blooms, the flowering stem dies down and divides the basal plate of the original bulb into two. Depending on the vigor of the plant and its age, this division will be more or less apparent. In time, the tissue between the two parts will perish, and two bulbs will function independently. Often, however, growers will seize the opportunity to split the dividing bulbs in the fall, some eight weeks after flowering. They crack open the divide by hand or plunge a knife down through the hole made where the defunct flower stem has twisted away.

Rhizomatous bulbs growing under good garden conditions can engender at least two new growing points from each original one. After a couple of seasons the whole rootstock can be divided using a knife, so that each new piece has a section of the old rhizome and at least one new growing point, distinguished by its paler scales. This can normally be done toward the end of summer.

The natural division of bulbs can cause overcrowded clusters in just a few seasons in garden conditions. The greater the competition between them, the less likely they are to grow into the fat high performers we desire. It therefore makes sense to lift and divide bulbs regularly, perhaps after one, two, or three seasons.

LIFTING BULBS

The time to lift bulbs is usually six weeks or so after blooming has ended, which means that most Asiatics can be dug in late summer. The tops may have been partially cut back to dispense with the dead flower heads (unless seed is to be collected) and the foliage, if not obviously faded or failing, will not be working efficiently, so the stems can be sacrificed and the bulbs shaken free of soil. There may well be a number of bulblets clasping the stem (see opposite).

Lifting bulbs is an opportunity to remove slugs and to cut away or tidy up any damaged scales. Cut surfaces should be treated with fungicide. The roots are almost useless, so loose ones can be removed, but the stronger ones can be useful to anchor the bulbs into their new homes. These bulbs will soon begin to make a new root system, which is the beginning of their annual growth cycle. Sometimes the new bulbs are dividing into two or more independent bulbs. These are easily pried apart by thrusting a knife point down the flower-stem hole into the basal

This raised bulb has several below-ground bulblets still attached to the stem.

The same bulb with the stem bulblets detached and all ready for planting.

plate. It is a matter of choice whether you do this or replant any multinosed bulbs as one. Bulbs are not meant to be out of the ground for any length of time, so you should replant them in the border or in pots immediately. If you cannot do this right away, store them in a container and cover them with peat or similar material which is damp, rather than wet, and place in a cool spot. Store the bulbs for no longer than is necessary. The aim is to encourage them to make a fresh extensive root system well before the onset of winter weather.

The Trumpets, Aurelians, many Orientals, and Orienpets are likely to bloom later than Asiatics, so a six-week period after blooming brings them closer to winter. But there should still be time to dig, divide, and replant so that the bulbs can re-establish themselves with strong root systems. If at lifting time the plants still look green and active, cut the stems to half their length and leave them on the bulbs. The shortened stems will return goodness to the bulbs and make useful handles when replanting. They also serve to mark the bulbs' positions in their new homes.

BELOW-GROUND STEM BULBLETS

Many lilies are dynamic procreators. A majority have at least some potential to produce bulblets on the portion of stem in the soil. The Asiatic group of species and all the Asiatic hybrids are particularly energetic in these endeavors, especially if the plants are growing vigorously. It is not unusual to see bulblet tips jostling together and pushing through the soil surface next to the stem. Their number and size can vary widely, from one to ten. LA hybrids can be extraordinarily prolific and may have bulblets as large as golf balls. Most others will be around the size of children's marbles, ranging down to minute ones not normally worth bothering with.

The six- to eight-week period after flowering can be an important time for these bulblets to fatten up for harvesting, usually when the main bulbs are lifted. Like the mother bulbs, they are best planted immediately; some will have already developed roots. If you plant them between the replanted main bulbs, one advantage is that the name of the plant is known, and another is that the cloned youngsters are in the same care regime as the parents, which will suit them as well. A possible disadvantage is that young plants could be swamped by the larger ones. If you do not want nonflowering young plants among your full-sized specimens, carefully label the bulblets and grow them on for a season in pots or nursery rows in a spare part of the garden. Most reasonably sized bulblets of Asiatics should have grown to flowering size after one growing season.

Martagon types can produce bulblets but are not noted for it. Trumpets will be less generous than Asiatics, though plants with Aurelian blood may be a little more free. Of the normal producers, stems that have had their potential flowering heads removed in infancy will often give more and larger bulblets.

LEAF-AXIL BULBILS

Lily species that produce bulbils in their leaf axils can be very generous, especially the tiger lily (*L. lancifolium*), the European *L. bulbiferum,* and a rare Asiatic Trumpet, *L. sargentiae. L. bulbiferum* has forms and clones that do not normally produce bulbils, including the best-known, *L. bulbiferum* var. *croceum.* Asiatic hybrids often have the potential to grow bulbils, too, and some will do this spontaneously, while others can be encouraged to perform by cutting off the flower head as soon as you see the small green flower buds developing. Often young, nonflowering bulbs will produce stems with a good number of bulbils.

The tiger lily bulbils are a dark purple where they receive sunlight, and each leaf axil may support one, two, or even three. As the stems are very leafy, each plant can have up to a hundred bulbils per stem. In the natural course of events these fall off as they ripen in the fall, by which stage they may already have started to grow roots and sometimes have a small leaf. The fallen bulbils plunge roots into the soil that pull the bulbils down, contracting accordian-like so to effect this process.

Bulbils can be harvested as they develop, from the end of summer to fall. The fat, ripe ones snap off easily, and younger ones can be left on for collection later. Plant them in drills in an open garden, as you might deal with vegetable seeds, or in pots or trays using a humus-rich but open, gritty commercial compost. Planted early, they will root readily and produce leaves so that plants are established before winter, when they will lose their foliage and mark time until spring. Planted in spring, they should grow strongly through the year, with most flowering the following summer.

CLONING FROM SCALES

This is a favorite bit of magic. It can be done at any time of the year, but the easiest period will be in very early spring, so that the resulting young plants can be grown on strongly through the growing year. Detach the scales and put them in a growing medium, either vermiculite or a gritty commercial potting mix (see opposite). Once the scales have produced embryo bulbs along their fractured edges, they can be potted up in pots or trays. Grow them on until each bulb has produced two or three leaves, at which stage the plants are probably ready to plant out in the open. If, when the scales are examined after the six- to eight-week gestation period, the bulbs look very small, they can be closed up again in their bags and given longer to fatten up.

In warm parts of the world where well-drained soils can be kept moist, scales can be detached and grown on outdoors in drills. Some bulbs, like the Martagons, have very brittle scales, and it is almost impossible to lift or handle them without some becoming detached. Left in the soil, these will form small bulbs without any leaves for the first year and will then increase in size over the seasons until they reach flowering size—a period that can be five years or longer.

1 Select a healthy bulb and break off scales close to the basal plate. With overlapping scales, it is easiest to work around the bulb until enough scales are detached. If it is a precious small bulb, you may have to be content with one or two, but a large bulb may yield six large scales without being drastically weakened. Discard slug-attacked, damaged, or apparently diseased scales.

2 Soak the scales in a systemic fungicide according to the maker's instructions but usually for 15–20 minutes. Give each group of scales a clearly written, indelible label.

3 You may now choose to enclose the scales in a plastic bag with a handful or two of moistened, clean vermiculite or similar inert material. Allow it to take up as much water as it can for 5 minutes, then drain before use. Close the bag, with plenty of air inside, and label it. Place each bag in a safe place (not necessarily in the dark) and keep at 65–70°F.

4 Alternatively, after soaking the scales in fungicide, insert them into a tray of gritty commercial potting mix with only the tip of each scale exposed. Label the tray, then soak it from below and allow to drain.

5 Enclose the tray in a plastic bag and seal to maintain a moist atmosphere. After 6–8 weeks, open the bag and pry up a scale or two to examine. They should have one to five embryo bulbs along their fractured bases. Each will have begun producing roots and possibly the first small leaf.

6 Introduce the little bulbs into gritty, humus-rich commercial potting mix in pots or trays. Plant a whole scale, with the bulbs 1 inch below the surface, or detach the bulbs and plant separately. Grow on until each has produced 2–3 leaves, at which point the plants are ready to pot up or plant out.

raising lilies from seed

There are a number of benefits to growing from seed. First, you can be sure that the plants are initially free from virus and other diseases. Among lily species there are some that are available only from seed. As a pod can easily contain 50–100 viable seeds, there is scope for a population explosion. There is always a chance of some variation within a species, so gardeners can play the evolutionary game and ensure "the survival of the fittest" as they envision it. Of course, hybrid seed can produce huge variations from a single pod of a self-fertilized cultivar. Controlled crosses stand a chance of combining the qualities that the breeder has in mind, but betting on the outcome is hazardous. There are lots of surprises, but while there are swans galore, ugly ducklings are extraordinarily rare.

There is normally a six- to eight-week period between successful pollination (see page 150) and seed ripening. The later the flowering season, the slower the seed ripens. Sometimes the late-ripening pods have to be cut and brought inside to be finished off, once it has become too wet and cold outdoors. Hang the cut stems upside down in a dry, airy, warm spot such as a sunroom or greenhouse. Lay sheets of newspaper below the stems to catch any seed that is released. Moisture is a particular danger to late-ripening pods, as fungus can attack them and its mycelium grows quickly through the pods, destroying the seed as it goes.

When the seed pods ripen, the tops crack open and the disk-like seed can be blown away. If you are going to be away from the garden at this time, it would be prudent to enclose the pods in muslin, held by rubber bands. The dry seed can be shelled out from the pods and the chaff lightly blown away. While chaff is without definition, viable seed is fatter. If a light is shone through the seed, the embryo can be clearly seen. How strongly you blow to remove the chaff without losing lively seed is a matter of judgment , but it is not that difficult.

Late-ripening seed pods have been brought under cover in the fall to continue ripening. Place a sheet of paper below the pods to catch any falling seed.

SOWING THE SEED

Seed needs moisture, warmth, and air to germinate, and this is usually provided by a seed-starting mix in a pot or tray. Damp vermiculite in a sealed bag or glass jar would also serve, and seed will even germinate on damp paper towels in a sealed plastic bag. Neither the vermiculite nor the paper provides any nourishment, so the germinated seedlings will have to be transferred to a suitable growing medium— a gritty, lime-free soil mix when the reserves from the seed run out. However, it is more usual to sow directly into such a mixture.

These flat, disk-like seeds are from a Trumpet lily, which produces larger seed than some smaller species and hybrids.

Seed can be sown immediately after harvesting or saved and dealt with at the end of winter or the very beginning of spring. Early ripened seed sown in late summer can germinate immediately to produce small bulbs and leaves before winter. These are best grown under glass in an airy atmosphere and sprayed with fungicide, otherwise fungus may cause damping-off and perhaps kill the tiny plants. The argument that because nature sows immediately this might be the course to follow is fairly compelling. Normally the safest place for seed is in the soil.

On the other hand, if seed is stored safely and sown in very early spring, the germinating seed and young plants will have the benefit of improving weather conditions, which should encourage steady, rapid growth without any of the checks that winter might conjure up. Good seed storage means enclosing the clean, dry seed with air in a sealed packet and keeping it cool—for example, in a domestic refrigerator (but not in the deep-freeze compartment).

GERMINATION

Seed germinates in several different ways, depending on the type of lily. Some begins to grow by sending out a shoot that develops a swelling at the end—this is the beginning of the bulb. The shoot curves, humps up to form a loop that breaks through the soil surface, and then pulls up its own free end to form a narrow strap-like "cotyledon" leaf, often with the seed case still attached at the end and waving aloft like a little flag. As the bulb grows, it gathers enough strength to send up its first true leaf, a spear-shaped one. This starting method is known as "epigeal" or "above-ground" germination.

The alternative method is called "hypogeal" or "below-ground" germination. These seeds produce a shoot that tends to descend perhaps 1 inch or so—and forms a tiny bulb, usually below the seed case. The food reserves stored in the seed are used to make the shoot and the beginnings of the little bulb with its first roots. When the roots start gathering nourishment, the bulb sends up its first leaf, a true spear-shaped one and not a cotyledon; this is the first sign of successful germination. With some kinds of lily, this single leaf is the total foliage for the duration of the first year.

Both the epigeal and hypogeal methods are further divided into those that germinate immediately—that is, within four to seven weeks—and those that delay matters, perhaps for a few months. Thus, we have four germinating categories (see the introduction to each species group in Choosing Species, beginning on page 40): epigeal immediate, epigeal delayed, hypogeal immediate, and hypogeal delayed. By far the largest categories are the epigeal immediate and the hypogeal delayed. Many gardeners will be sowing more of the epigeal immediate types than of any others, and luckily these are the most straightforward.

The way we manage our seed can depend on its germination method. In the absence of any other advice, seeds are best sown as soon after harvest or purchase as possible, since seed that is not properly stored will begin to lose its vitality.

SOWING TIMES FOR ALL CATEGORIES

Epigeal immediate and hypogeal immediate Seed harvested early may be sown immediately and should provide small bulbs before winter. Seed saved in fall or later is best kept dry and cool until the end of winter, then sown. Give each seed about 1 square inch of space, and keep it moist rather than wet. Use a fungicide spray early on. Seed sown in spring should start growing quickly and produce progressively more leaves, making a rosette of these before attempting to produce a stem (this usually happens in the second season). When leaves start to turn yellow in fall, the bulbs of vigorous kinds can be 1 inch or more in diameter. The aim is to grow a bulb large enough to plant out in a nursery row or permanent flowering position by fall. Slower growers can be kept just moist in pots over winter and grown on for a further year before planting out.

Really strong kinds, such as *L. regale,* can be sown outside in early spring in temperate climates, and some bulbs may be big enough to have a flower in their second year if grown well.

Epigeal delayed Sow seed straight from the pods or keep until the end of winter. Some batches may germinate together, but others may start into growth at intervals. You can abandon the nursery pots when enough plants have emerged and been pricked out.

Hypogeal delayed The main types that behave in this way are the Orientals and the Martagons. The seeds need an initial 12-week period of relative warmth—say, 70°F—during which time they will form tiny bulbs. These then need six weeks of cool conditions, preferably just above freezing, to break the bulbs' dormancy and trigger the formation of the first leaves. Seeds sown in the fall and kept warm will therefore be ready for their cool period by the end of winter and should be producing leaves at the beginning of spring. The plants should then grow away through spring and summer.

L. martagon, with its relatives and hybrids, ripens seed early. If this is sown after harvesting, it will receive the warm period naturally, followed by the cool of winter, and will then be ready to display its first leaves in spring. The seed of Martagons is usually plentiful; it can be sown in weed-free cultivated soil in the open. Even if a proportion of the seed is lost to natural hazards, there will still be plenty of survivors.

1 Sow seed in pots at the end of winter, using a mixture made up of topsoil or loam—or a humus-based mixture combined with equal parts grit or washed coarse sand. Commercial seed-starting mixes may be safest. Fill the pots to within 1 inch of the top, sow the seed at roughly half–inch intervals and cover with at least another half–inch layer of grit.

2 Soak the pots in water, then drain and enclose in a plastic bag, or plunge them up to their rims in the soil in a bed or border outside and cover with plastic or glass. Fast-germinating seed ("immediate") will show through in 4–7 weeks, whereas delayed kinds may not appear until the following year.

3 Grow the seedlings on for a year or two within the nursery pot or until they form a stem. Plant out in early spring or early fall into well-drained soil, and keep moist during dry periods up to the end of fall. It is not exceptional to have the first flowers from *L. amabile, L. pumilum, L. regale, L. formosanum,* and *L. longiflorum* in their second season.

Seed of Orientals can be late ripening and may be sown in pots at the beginning of winter, as already suggested. Alternatively, find some clean jars with screw-cap tops to use as incubators. Moisten some vermiculite with clean water, then drain away the surplus before placing a handful or two inside the jar. Soak seed of Orientals overnight in clean water to wash away any natural germination inhibitors. Place the seed and a label in the container. Shake it, with the top secured, and stick another label on the outside. Make sure some of the seed is at the edge of the jar so that its progress can be observed after placing the containers in a warmish spot at around 70°F.

After about three months, small bulbs will be seen. When these are fully formed and beginning to produce roots, you can remove them and pot them up into a gritty lime-free commercial potting mix. Place the pots in a cool spot in the open or in a cold frame or unheated greenhouse. When leaves appear, give the pots a little more warmth and keep them reasonably moist. Alternatively, give the little bulbs in their glass containers their cool period *in situ*. Once root and leaf growth have begun, prick out the young bulbs when there is a leaf big enough to handle.

breeding new lilies

This is something that anyone can do successfully—the process is simple and the rewards are great. As the professional breeders have their eyes firmly fixed on the value of good cut flowers, it must be hoped that some of the rejects of their breeding programs—kinds with outward-facing or pendent flowers—can be passed into the garden bulb trade. It is with flowers of such habits that amateur breeders could do stalwart work. Even if new seedlings never get beyond the garden fence, the pleasure to be obtained from raising new kinds is very special. Fortunately it is almost impossible to raise an ugly lily.

Cultivars will often have a complicated heredity, and self-pollinated seed may give rise to seedlings that do not look much like the seed parent, but there will be features that are similar even if they are only leaf form, height, and flowering period. The gardener may view cultivars and think how one could be improved in certain respects by the input of genetic material from another. Cross-pollination may give the desired effect or may produce surprises with new combinations of features.

THE TECHNIQUE

Lily anthers usually produce large quantities of pollen, so these should be removed to prevent self-pollination (see opposite). The stigmas become sticky when they are at their most receptive—usually a day or so after the flower has opened—so this is the time to carry out hand pollination. If the chosen parents are not blooming at the same time, you can save pollen from the earlier flower for later use. Remove anthers before the pollen has been lost, and store them in clean plastic containers such as film canisters or pill bottles. If the anthers are fresh they will be damp, so leave the containers open until the anthers have fully dried. Then seal them and store in a refrigerator, carefully labeled. Pollen will keep for weeks or even months in such conditions.

Once the flowers are pollinated, label with clearly written labels. It is usual to write the name of the seed parent first, so that a label might read 'Sorbet' x Lollipop', where 'Sorbet' is the seed parent whose stigmas have received the 'Lollipop' pollen. While most pollination can take place in the garden, bulbs may be potted up and the crossing conducted under glass. An advantage is that the flowers will come earlier, and any resulting seed will ripen much sooner. The warmer, more humid conditions may also help facilitate fertilization.

The laws of inheritance obtain in the lily family, and experience will give some guide as to the likely outcomes of a breeding exercise. In the simplest case, a characteristic will be governed by a single gene with two forms (alleles). Spots on the flowers could be governed by such a gene, one form favoring spotted flowers and the other spotless ones. An Asiatic lily inheriting genes from both parents favoring spots will obviously have spotted offspring. If a pair of spotless genes is

POLLINATING LILIES BY HAND

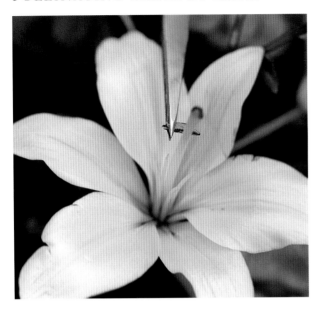

To prevent self-pollination, remove the anthers by hand or by using tweezers, preferably before they have split and begun to release their pollen.

Dust the prominent stigma all over with the foreign pollen, either by dragging an anther of the pollen parent over the stigma surface or by transferring some pollen to it using a small watercolor brush.

inherited, the flower will be spot-free. But if a plant inherits both gene forms, the flowers will be spotted because in this case the one favoring spots is "dominant," while the spotless is "recessive." A spotted individual carrying a recessive gene for the spotless state will pass this on through half its egg cells and half its pollen grains. If this individual is self-fertilized, the recessive effect will be revealed only if one recessive gene links up with a similar one—a one-in-four chance.

BREEDING PLANS

Even in the smallest-scale breeding operation it pays to have a clear idea of your aims. As a single pod can contain 50–100 seeds, it is important to show discretion. New possibilities will tempt further experimentation each season, so that you may soon have a large number of plants at various stages. Some kinds will take longer than others to reach flowering-sized bulbs. Asiatics sown in late winter and well grown may have their first blooms in midsummer the following year, while some Trumpets may bloom after two years' growth.

There are endless possibilities for small-scale raisers. LAs and Asiatics that face out or down are relatively scarce and may be thought more graceful than the numerous upward kinds. And while most Asiatics are without scent, a few are gently perfumed; gardeners would enjoy a series of scented novelties.

Consider the use of species lilies such as *L. pumilum* to provide dainty, many-headed spikes of flowers. *L. amabile* and its yellow form, *L. amabile* var. *luteum*, together with the small *L. concolor*, may be used to add brilliance to the surface sheen of petals. These are species with good disease resistance to impart to seedlings. There is still something to be gained by using *L. bulbiferum* with its very early flowering habit and indifference to alkalinity, while *L. dauricum* and *L. wilsonii* have distinctive flowers and are easily crossed with a wide range of mates, the first imparting a robust constitution and often early blooms to seedlings. Pendent flowers may be bred from such species as *L. pumilum, L. davidii,* and *L. lancifolium.*

Gardeners can never get enough of the Martagon-type hybrids, and this is just the field where the amateur could surge ahead. The use of the unusual tangerine *L. tsingtauense,* with upward-facing flowers and polished surfaces, could widen the range of possibilities among the Martagons.

appendix

classification of lily species

Comber's widely respected classification of 1949 gives us seven groups: Martagon, North American, Candidum, Oriental, Asian, Trumpet, and Dauricum. The Martagons are seen as the most primitive types, the closest to the prototype *Lilium*, followed by the North Americans. The classification is based on various factors listed in order of their adjudged importance.

Germination
(a) hypogeal (above-ground)
(b) epigeal (below-ground)
(a) delayed—after some months (b) immediate—after four to seven weeks

Leaf arrangement
(a) whorled, i.e. rings of leaves at the same level (b) scattered

Bulb scales
(a) jointed (b) entire

Seed weight
(a) heavy (b) light

Bulb shape and habit
(a) erect (b) sub-rhizomatous
(c) rhizomatous
(d) stoloniferous

Petals
(a) papillose—with raised points (b) smooth

Nectary
(a) pubescent, i.e. with soft hairs
(b) glabrous, i.e. hairless

Flower form
(a) Turk's cap (b) trumpet

Bulb color
(a) white (b) purple

Stem habit
(a) erect (b) stoloniform

Leaf stalks
(a) petiole, i.e. obvious stalk
(b) obscure or none

Stigma
(a) large (b) small

Stem roots
(a) present (b) absent

Stems per bulb
(a) one (b) sometimes more

additional species
to those described in the main text (pages 42–67)

OTHER MARTAGON SPECIES (Group 1)

L. distichum This species, from central Korea, northeast China, and neighboring territories grows in woodland soils in cool conditions. It has a few horizontal or slightly downward-tilted flowers on stems that can reach an exceptional 3 feet, but are more often half this. Well-endowed stems can have a dozen blooms. Foliage is confined to a single whorl with perhaps a few scattered leaves above. Narrow petals spread outward before recurving only at the tips. Their color is tangerine to pale red, maybe with a few beauty spots.

L. medeoloides Also from Korea and surrounding countries, this species is very obviously a Martagon type, but this is the mini version, with stems having only one whorl of leaves and normally under 2 feet in stature. Pendent flowers have petals curved back but not so extremely as the team leader, and their color is a rich tangerine with dark spots; there are red forms too. It needs an open, humus-rich soil.

OTHER N. AMERICAN SPECIES (Group 2)

Group 2a
L. bolanderi From 18 inches to 4 feet, the slender wiry stems carry a few flowers of an unusual deep burgundy-red in the best forms, and there are others of a rather muddier orange-red. Funnel-shaped blooms are held horizontally or slightly downward with petal tips just recurving.

L. columbianum This is a widely distributed species, usually growing to around 3 feet high, with medium-sized bright orange flowers spotted maroon. Colors can vary, with some all-red ones. Usually generous with nodding flowers. Relatively easy to grow from seed but not necessarily long-lived.

L. humboldtii This resembles the tiger lily but with orthodox N. American whorled leaves. Nodding Turk's caps are golden orange, heavily spotted maroon except at the tips, the spots sometimes being ringed in gold. This is a stronger species than many and capable of 30 or more flowers to a good stem.

L. rubescens Rare and like *L. washingtonianum* but with the bells swung upright. Half of each petal forms the bell; the other half points out to make a star shape. It usually opens white but becomes flushed with pinkish mauve in its prime, then turns a senescent purple before dying off. A light peppering with purple in the base is an optional extra that in some forms is taken almost to excess and invades the whole flower. There are no golden rules for success, but a start should be made with very good drainage and an open-structured soil.

L. washingtonianum Rare in cultivation, this has horizontally held white trumpet blooms dotted with the purple that may also be staining the base.

Group 2b
L. maritimum Another coastal species from farther south than *L. occidentale* (see below). Red-orange spotted flowers are fairly gently recurved.

L. nevadense Found inland in California and Nevada, this species looks like a half-sized relative of *L. pardalinum,* but it has a scent.

L. occidentale This grows in a strip of land along the Pacific Coast of northern California and southern Oregon, where it is under threat from increasing human activity. Bulbs make their home on hummocks of soil that protrude from wet, boggy areas. Nodding red flowers with orange and green bases have much-recurved petals. Height 2–5 feet.

L. parryi Rather lightweight whorls of foliage as well as scattered leaves clothe wiry stems 2½ft–5 feet high, carrying ten or more wide golden bell-trumpet flowers, usually without any hint of orange. I have counted 80 on an exceptionally crowded stem.

L. parvum This species grows in the hills behind the distribution of *L. occidentale* and *L. maritimum.* Small horizontal bells are usually a rich orange that gives way to gold and a green center. Bell-shaped blooms hang as buds, then swing up to the horizontal as they open. There are 12–25 flowers to a 4–6-foot stem.

L. vollmeri A *pardalinum*-type plant built on more slender lines, the 2–3-foot stems are well furnished with whorls of slender leaves. Six or more typical Turk's caps are vivid tangerine dotted maroon-red but with golden throats. Formerly listed as *L. roezlii.*

L. wigginsii Hailing from the wooded mountainsides of Oregon and California, this is a pleasing plant that is not impossible in the garden, although it is not necessarily a dangerous land-grabber. It has upright leaves on dark-green stems 2–5 feet tall. A pyramid of nodding amber flowers may number 10–25, with tiny purple spots overall. Petals and leaves are slender, giving the whole plant a daintier feel than some. Needs cool, humus-rich soil.

Group 2c
L. carolinianum (syn. *L. michauxii*) This is rarely seen in cultivation; neither bulbs nor seeds are readily available. The species grows in dry, well-drained soils in the Southeast. Stoloniferous bulbs produce stems 1–3 feet, with whorls of relatively broad lanceolate leaves waved at the margins. One to five hanging, scented flowers are of typical *pardalinum* form and shine in shades of orange-red but with pale yellow throats. It is a stem rooter that prefers neutral or soil of humus-enriched sand.

L. iridollae This is a very rarely grown species with tiny bulbs and small golden flowers with much recurved petals. It is unusual in producing a cluster of narrow basal leaves after blooming and keeping these through the winter in the manner of *L. candidum.* It grows 1.5–4 feet tall.

L. michiganense A widespread species with showy, waxy,

orange-red flowers heavily spotted on the lower two-thirds of the petals. Like *L. canadense*, it has long sloping pedicels, and just at the end these turn down to have the blooms in a fully pendent pose. They start with a funnel shape before recurving sharply. There may be three to seven stems, 4–5 feet tall, on an established plant, but exceptional ones will number a few dozen. Like its relatives, the stoloniferous bulbs enjoy a deep humus-rich soil; it is reported to be alkaline-tolerant.

Group 2d
L. catesbaei A tiny little tuft of a bulb supports a mini stem of 9–18 inches, with leaves arranged alternately and more or less clasping the stem. An upward-facing flower is relatively large, with petals having narrow hafts so that you can see through the flower; the petals spread and recurve gently at the tips. This is an awkward plant that produces a tiny rosette of narrow leaves in the autumn to be cared for through the winter; not an easy garden plant.

L. philadelphicum A small, dainty wild flower that is only fleetingly known in cultivation. Stems grow 1.5–3 feet tall, with whorled foliage and scattered leaves. The upward-facing flowers are red-orange, spotted golden at the base; the petals point outward from these goblet bases.

OTHER CANDIDUM SPECIES (Group 3)

Group 3b
L. carniolicum An alpine species with chunky Turk's cap flowers of rusty red. Half a dozen flowers can be held by a 1.5–3-foot stem, the scattered leaves being a little hairy along their margins and the veins on the lower side. *L. carniolicum albanicum*, a smaller plant with lemon or golden flowers, has been given specific, sub-specific, and varietal status at different times; perhaps it is simplest to regard it as a variety. *L. carniolicum jankae* is another variation, but with yellow or orange flowers.

L. ciliatum Once confused with *L. pyrenaicum* and other species, this plant hails from northern Turkey. Large bulbs produce stems 2–5 feet tall, clothed with long, narrow leaves that are rough to the touch and margined with hairs. Flowers are ivory or primrose-yellow, but with a purplish center and a light spray of tiny dots. The hanging flowers have recurving petals, but the shape is wider than the restricted Turk's caps of *L. pyrenaicum*. This is an interesting species, without any special garden merit beyond that of others.

L. pomponium A pleasing species from the Maritime Alps, with stems 1–2½ feet tall, with generous amounts of grassy, narrow leaves and dainty heads of one to ten smallish nodding Turk's caps. These are firm-textured, lightly peppered with tiny dots and bright red-orange but without the lacquer finish of *L. chalcedonicum*.

Group 3c
L. polyphyllum A species from the Himalayas that seems ill-equipped for cultivation since it dislikes wet winters. Reports of stems 7 feet tall with up to 30 flowers certainly whet the appetite, though more normal endeavors are around 4 feet, with six flowers. Hanging blooms are ivory-white outside but creamy inside, with a more or less mauve blush and lengthwise streaks of mauve-purple. The petals make a funnel before opening out and perhaps recurving a little.

OTHER ORIENTAL SPECIES (Group 4)

Group 4c
L. japonicum A lovely wide pink trumpet species. The wiry stems have slender, dark leaves and usually carry one to three heavily perfumed flowers, held horizontally.

L. nobilissimum This is a white trumpet species from one of the southern Japanese islands. Flowers are 4 inches across and deep, their pure white being enhanced by a green exterior and golden anthers. It can have up to six perfumed blooms to a stem 2½–4 feet tall. In temperate climates this is likely to be a greenhouse plant.

Group 4d
L. brownii This looks like the traditional white trumpet lily, and rather a special one at that, but it is in fact an Oriental with *L. speciosum* and *L. auratum* as its disparate relatives. Its 3–4-foot sloping stems are well clothed with narrow leaves, and above these come the very large, dark mahogany buds. The open flowers are sparkling white with golden throats and chocolate anthers that soon become golden with pollen. There are forms with paler pinkish buds, rather than chocolate. The form *L. brownii* var. *australe* is usually the most vigorous and can double the standard height. Its buds may be greenish, its flowers are as large or larger than the species, while its foliage may be even narrower. I have enjoyed periods of success with this species—but alas all too short. The bulbs, composed of many narrow scales, seem to be quite vigorous for a while, then unaccountably fail—but perhaps other gardeners will be luckier.

OTHER ASIAN SPECIES (Group 5)

Group 5a
L. papilliferum A rare species in cultivation, a smallish plant that might suggest one of the dark forms of *L. martagon* in its flowers, though the leaves are scattered. It grows some 18 inches high in normal circumstances, but is able to double this. Petals are tightly curled back, the color a deep maroon that veers toward an eggplant-colored darkness, against which the orange anthers look exuberant. It has up to four or five very fragrant flowers. Grows in soils from alkaline to mildly acid. One of the last to appear above ground and a late bloomer, perhaps opening at the end of summer.

Group 5b
L. amabile This is one of the easier species in cultivation and one of many that have been involved in the breeding of Asiatic hybrids. Nodding Martagon-shaped flowers of red with black dots are hung from stems 1.5–3 feet tall. Plenty of bulblets, especially from around the less stout stems.

L. callosum Slender but strong stems reach as high as 3–4 feet and carry perhaps five or six flowers. These are tightly curled balls that open later than in many species. The color is a rather matte red but brighter orange when open. The shortish flower stalks make the flower heads somewhat narrow. It is not difficult to grow from seed, though we have not found it a particularly long-lived plant. There is a yellow form, *L. callosum* var. *flaviforum*.

L. cernuum Nodding Turk's caps in a lavender-tinged pink with a paler center where there will be a few small spots. Narrow leaves furnish wiry stems reaching 18–30 inches high. A dainty plant with a few flowers to each stem, this species is the important source of the pink coloring in Asiatic hybrids. An alkaline-tolerant bulb that grows quickly from seed.

L. concolor This dinky little lily is an unusual Asiatic in having flowers that open as wide stars and look frankly upward. The color is a bright rich orange similar to that of *L. pumilum*. The erect stems are only 12–16 inches high and rarely carry more than three or four of the wide-pointing stars. The bulbs are usually about the size of marbles. It is a sturdy and pleasing plant which grows quickly from seed, that is well worth sowing, as it may be short-lived.

L. fargesii A slender plant, rather similar to *L. callosum* but of no particular horticultural merit. Nodding greenish-white flowers with dark lilac spots, often single but possibly two to six on stems 2 feet tall. Petals much reflexed from the short expanded throats. Thin, scattered leaves.

L. pumilum Long grown as *L. tenuifolium*, this jolly little plant has small bulbs not much bigger than marbles, formed of a few tightly compacted scales. It has erect stems 1–2 feet high, though, exceptionally, almost double this, clasped by narrow, grassy leaves. Depending on the strength of the bulb, you can rejoice in up to 20 rounded balls of diligently polished vermilion. One can almost guarantee flowers from even very small bulbs. It is a hardy little plant and will persist for a few seasons if not allowed to seed itself to death. Obviously this is nature's way of perpetuating the species, found in Siberia, across northeastern parts of Russia, and into northern China.

Group 5c

L. amoenum Nearly a *Nomocharis*. Little bulbs produce stems up to 12 inches high, with one to three pendent cups of mauve-pink. Rarely grown in gardens.

L. bakerianum On that difficult border of the genus elbowing toward the *Nomocharis* and *Fritillaria* genera. An awkward, rarely grown, stoloniferous-stemmed bulb from upper Burma and western China, growing to only 1–2$\frac{1}{2}$ feet high. The nodding, swinging trumpet-bells are ivory-white, suffused with green on the outside and inside spotted mahogany.

L. exanthum Only some 8 inches high and like a fritillary. A single yellow or lime-colored bell is hung out. Enthusiasts are trying this in cultivation, but it is unlikely to be easy. In nature it grows in dry rhododendron moorland.

L. henricii Another with leanings toward the *Nomocharis*. A rare kind that does better in cool, acid soils which do not get dry in the growing period but are also not subject to stagnant water. Wide bells of long

pointed petals brought a little upward from the completely pendulous; pale pink or a light rosy purple. 2–3 feet tall.

L. nanum Of all tiny lilies from the highlands of Upper Burma, western China, Nepal, Sikkim, and similar areas, *L. nanum* is the most often found in cultivation. The other species will challenge the most expert grower and are never likely to be widely grown or readily available garden plants, but *L. nanum* is a favorite with alpine enthusiasts. Stems 6 inches tall have several grassy leaves and a single nodding, open, pointed flower of shining chocolate-flavored maroon. The color varies; there are mauve and pink forms, and *L. nanum* var. *flavidum* has soft yellow nodding blooms. Needs a gritty, well-drained soil.

L. paradoxum One of the rarest species, found only in small numbers growing in screes in two passes of southeast Tibet. At present it is not in cultivation. It is as close to the *Nomocharis* genus as a lily can get without losing its papers. It stands 8–18 inches tall, with two to four whorls of foliage and one or two scattered leaves below. Nodding flowers are like a checker lily in form—with no recurving of the petals. The color is a dark red with somber purple admixture especially on the outside; "rich mahogany" is a good description.

L. primulinum This is akin to *L. nepalense* but taller at 3–6 feet, and so far apparently less amenable to cultivation. It has the same thick-textured flowers, usually yellowish green but generously overpainted with dark maroon in the center. Variable in height, flower size,

and coloring; there are even forms with none of the central purple that is normally considered the hallmark of the species. Leaves can measure up to 5 inches long and 1 inch wide. Petals of the larger forms may be 4–5 inches long if stretched flat, but their habit is to recurve strongly.

L. semperviviodeum A tiny plant similar to *L. amoenum*. One or two hanging bells of white, but spotted crimson and hung from stems only 6 inches high.

L. sherriffiae A rarity that could easily be mistaken for a fritillaria. Stems 1–2 feet tall have one or two hanging bells with fritillaria colors and markings: dark brown and purple outside, checkered lime-yellow inside.

L. soulieli Discovered in 1898 and not grown successfully in cultivation since. Though seed has been raised on occasion, the young plants tend to die away. It was first described as a fritillaria, a plant standing 8–18 inches high, with deep crimson-purple nodding flowers. These are fragrant and normally solitary, but twins can occur. Petals measure 1 inch.

OTHER TRUMPET SPECIES (Group 6)

Group 6a

L. sargentiae Glistening white trumpets opening after *L. regale*. Rare, especially in cultivation, and difficult to maintain in the garden. Buds usually purple, but some more green than purple; flowers sometimes with a whispered pink suggestion as a shadow from the outside pigment. This lily produces bulbils in the leaf axils.

L. sulphureum Another late trumpet, a rarity in cultivation, with large, pale yellow flowers. Prone to virus attack.

Group 6b

L. brownii Botanically *L. brownii* is classified with the Oriental group of species, but as far as the gardener is concerned, it is another white Trumpet. It is listed above under its botanical relatives.

L. formosanum From Taiwan (formerly known as Formosa), this is a variable species. Plants close to the shoreline are relatively tall and have been measured up to 6 feet high, but as the species makes its way up the hill slopes it shrinks until it is diminished to an elfin size, perhaps only 6 inches tall. At whatever stature, the flowers are of the same form, very narrow in the throat but widely expanded at the mouth. Buds are usually dark purple-maroon, but the open blooms are white with golden throats, though often you can detect a shadow of the outer coloring, as if looking through fine bone china. The dwarf forms, named *L. formosanum* var. *pricei*, are the ones most often seen in cultivation. There is something of the clown about the wiry stems, narrow foliage, and quite surprisingly large trumpet heads, one to a stem. I have had bulbs performing outside with no attention for several years, blooming not very many weeks after *L. regale*.

L. neilgherrense An interesting species, in that it is found in the hills of southern India, though rarely, and is the closest any lily gets to the equator. In most areas it would be a greenhouse plant with large

white trumpets with lemon-yellow throats. All-yellow forms have been noted.

L. philippinense Another of the island Trumpets. White trumpet flowers, sometimes flushed purple in bud and greenish at the base inside. Standing 1–3 feet tall.

L. wallichianum A very late-flowering kind, not too tall, that makes an useful plant to grow in a pot. Smallish bulbs come into growth late, and under unheated glass will often wait until fall before coming into full flower. It has very proper, finely textured white trumpets with chaste narrow bases that give way to wide mouths and can look very charming. A species found in the Himalayas and not difficult under glass, where it will increase quickly.

THE DAURICUM GROUP (Group 7)

L. dauricum, L. maculatum, L. wilsonii

Characteristics: germination above-ground immediate, scattered leaves with leaf stalks, jointed scales, papillose petals, nectary with hairs, erect flowers, erect white bulbs, stoloniferous stems with roots

L. dauricum This is the name of a species or a form of *L. maculatum,* which by the rules of nomenclature precedence should correctly be called *L. pennsylvanicum*—a confusing name for a Japanese plant. The usual flowers are upward-facing, wide bowls with the concave petals showing no reflexing; the tips may stretch out more widely in forms such as the diminutive *L. maculatum dauricum* var. *alpinum*. What is grown in Europe as the typical plant is a vigorous one that grows rapidly from seed. It blooms early in the season, bearing large flowers of rich tangerine-orange and some gold but well speckled overall. It displays notable air gaps in the center of the flowers where the petals narrow toward the stem.

L. maculatum This name appears more frequently as *L.* × *maculatum* in lily literature and covers a collection of hybrid lilies originally derived from Japanese species. It has now been rehabilitated as a specific name for a species found quite widely in Japan with upward-facing blooms with petals that narrow toward the stem. Petal tips can reflex. The colors are a mix of orange and tangerine, heavily freckled with dark maroon.

L. wilsonii This may be no more than a late-flowering form of *L. maculatum*, but the flowers are paler, often apricot colored, and up to 6 inches wide. The color is variable, *L. wilsonii* var. *flavum* being used as the name for buttercup-yellow or sulfur-colored forms, these being spotted maroon and with the petal centers suffused deeper gold or tangerine.

classification of hybrid lilies

The large number of lily hybrids has been classified to make them more manageable. We follow that recommended by the Royal Horticultural Society, which broadly mirrors the species classification.

Division I
Hybrids derived from such species or hybrid groups as *L. lancifolium, L. cernuum, L. davidii, L. leichtlinii, L.* × *maculatum, L.* × *hollandicum, L. amabile, L. pumilum, L. concolor, L. bulbiferum*
(a) with upright flowers
(b) with outward-facing flowers
(c) with pendent flowers

Division II
Hybrids of the Martagon type of which one parent has been a form of *L. martagon* or *L. hansonii*

Division III
Hybrids derived from *L. candidum, L. chalcedonicum,* and related European species (but excluding *L. martagon*)

Division IV
Hybrids of North American species

Division V
Hybrids derived from *L. longiflorum* and *L. formosanum* without any admixture

Division VI
Hybrid Trumpet lilies and Aurelian hybrids derived from Asiatic species including *L. henryi* but excluding those derived from *L. auratum, L. speciosum, L. japonicum,* and *L. rubellum*
(a) with trumpet-shaped flowers
(b) with bowl-shaped and outward-facing flowers
(c) with flat flowers
(d) with distinctly recurved flowers

Division VII
Hybrids of Far Eastern species such as *L. auratum, L. speciosum, L. japonicum,* and *L. rubellum,* including any of their hybrids with *L. henryi*

(a) with trumpet-shaped flowers
(b) with bowl-shaped flowers
(c) with flat flowers
(d) with recurved flowers

Division VIII
All hybrids not found in Divisions I–VII

false lilies
Many other plants produce flowers that resemble lilies in some way and their common names allude to this. The most common are listed below, with their botanical names, to help prevent confusion.

Common name	Genus/species	Common name	Genus/species	Common name	Genus/species
African corn lily	*Ixia*	Daylily	*Hemerocallis*	Torch lily	*Kniphofia*
African lily	*Agapanthus*	Foxtail lily	*Eremurus*	Trout lily	*Erythronium*
Amazon lily	*Eucharis x grandiflora*	Giant lily	*Doryanthes excelsa*	Voodoo lily	*Sauromatum venosum*
Atamasco lily	*Zephranthes atamasco*	Ginger lily	*Hedychium coronarium*	Water lily	*Nuphar + Nymphaea*
Belladonna lily	*Amaryllis belladonna*	Guernsey lily	*Nerine sarniensis*	Wood lily	*Lilium philadelphicum + Trillium*
Blackberry lily	*Belamcanda chinensis*	Lily of the valley	*Convallaria*	Zephyr lily	*Zephranthes grandiflora*
Bluehead lily	*Clintonia borealis*	Peruvian lily	*Alstroemeria*		
Calla lily	*Zantedeschia*	Plantain lily	*Hosta*		
Camass lily	*Camassia*	Scarborough lily	*Cyrtanthus elatus*		
Checker lily	*Fritillaria meleagris*	Spear lily	*Doryanthes excelsa*		
Climbing lily	*Gloriosa superba*	Toad lily	*Tricyrtis*		

further information

Sources of seeds

NORTH AMERICAN LILY SOCIETY (see page 157) *Seed list*

CHILTERN SEEDS, Bortree Stile, Ulverston, Cumbria LA12 7PB, ENGLAND, UK *Seeds of a wide range of species and some hybrid strains*

RHS LILY GROUP (see page 157) *Seed list*

ALPINE GARDEN SOCIETY AGS Centre, Avonbank, Pershore, Worcestershire, WR10 3JP, UK
tel 01386 554790
ags@alpinegardensociety.org
seed list

Sources of bulbs

United States

AMBERGATE GARDENS
8151 Krey Ave
Waconia, MN 55387-9616
tel/fax (612) 443-2248 *Species*

ARROWHEAD ALPINES
PO Box 857
Fowlerville, MI 48836 *Species*

AUTUMN GLADE BOTANICALS
46857 W. Ann Arbor Trail
Plymouth, MI 48170
tel (313) 480-4675
fax (313) 459-2604 *Species*

B & D LILIES
284566 Hwy 101S, PO Box 2007, Port Townsend, WA 98368,
tel (360) 765-4341
fax (360) 765-4074
www. lilybulb.com.
Extensive list, many exclusive

BARNHAVEN GARDENS
1920 Landing Road
Mt. Vernon, WA 98273
tel (360) 466-5805
fax (360) 466-1404

BORBELETA GARDENS INC.
15980 Canby Ave
Faribault, MN 55021
tel (507) 334-2807
fax (507) 334-0365
Some exclusive listings

THE BULB CRATE
2560 Deerfield Road
Riverwoods, IL 60015
tel (847) 317-1414
fax (847) 317-1417
abulb@aol.com

CALIFORNIA NURSERY
PO Box 515
Oregon House, CA 95962,
Species

ELYSIAN FIELDS
PO Box 1636
Springfield, MO 22151-0636
tel (703) 503-0032

FOGBELT GROWERS
5096 Dows Prairie Road
McKinleyville, CA 95519,
fax (707) 839-1364
fogbelt@ humboldt1.com
www.fogbeltgrowers.com
Oriental hybrids

THE ENCHANTED LILY GARDEN
12827 164th Ave, NE
Redmond, WA 98052
tel (206) 883-7318

HARTLE-GILMAN GARDENS
RR#4, Box 272
Owatonna, MN 55060
tel (507) 451-3191
fax (507) 455-0087
Asiatics, Martagons, species

HERONSWOOD NURSERY LTD.
7530 NE 288th St.
Kingston, WA 983446-9502
Species

J & P BULBS
4141 234th Ave.
St. Francis, MN 55070
lilybulbs@webtv.net

JACQUES AMAND
PO Box 59001

Potomac, MD 20859
tel (800) 452-5414
fax (301) 762-2943 *Species*

THE LILY GARDEN
4902 NE 147th Ave.
Vancouver, WA 98629
tel (360) 253-6275
thelilygdn@aol.com
Judith Freeman breeder and grower; pioneer embryo culture

THE LILY PAD
3403 Steamboat Is. Rd NW
Olympia, WA 98502
tel (360) 866-0291
info@lilypsdbulbs.com
www.lilypadbulbs.com

MAK-LEEK INC.
39100 Ridge Drive
Scio, OR 97374
tel (503) 394-4455
fax (503) 394-4444
plntblbs@wvi.com

MAPLE LEAF NURSERY
4236 Greenstone Road
Placerville, CA 95667 *Species*

MARLBORO BULB INC.
2524 Castle Hayne Road
Wilmington, NC 28401-3357
tel (910) 762-5609
fax (910) 762-4148

OLD HOUSE GARDENS
536 Third Street
Ann Arbor, MI 48103-4957
tel (734) 995-1486
fax (734) 995-1687
OHGBulbs@aol.com

PARK SEED CO.
1 Parkton Ave
Greenwood, SC 29647-0001
tel (800) 845-3369
fax (864) 941-4206
www.parkseed.com

VAN BOURGONDIEN
PO Box 1000
Babylon, NY 11702-0598
tel (800) 662-9997
www. dutchbulbs.com

WAYSIDE GARDENS
Hodges. SC 29695-0001
tel (800) 845-1124
fax (800) 457-9712
Wide selection

Canada

AMBROSIA GARDENS
PO Box 1135, Vernon, BC, VIT, 6N4, Canada
tel/fax (250) 766-1394
ambrosia@silk.net
www.silk.net/personal/ambrosia/index.htm

BRECK'S
Port Burwell,
ON NOJ 1TO, Canada
tel (800) 644-5505
www.brecks.com

FOX LILY RANCH
RR#2, Millet, AB, TOC 1ZO, Canada
tel/fax (403) 387-4382
Hybridizer, Asiatics, speciality Martagons

GRATRIX GARDEN LILIES
PO Box 186, Coldwater, ON, LOK 1EO, Canada
tel (705) 835-6794
gratlily@ beconnex.net
www.beconnex.net/-gratlily

HILLCREST HARMONY FLOWERS
Box 24, Churchbridge, SK, SOA OMO, Canada
tel (306) 896-2992
putld@ sk.sympatico.ca
www.pacific-pages.com/putld/lilies.htm
Supplies only in Canada; includes lilies bred in Saskatchewan

HOLLANDIA FLOWERS & BULBS
PO Box 36, Site 219, RR#2, Carvel, AB, TOE OHO Canada
tel (780) 963-8153
oranje@telusplanet.net
www.parklandebusiness.com/hollandia/

HORNER LILIES
23505 Valleyview Road, Thorndale, ON, NOM 2PO,

Canada
tel (519) 461-0492

LISA'S LILY GARDEN
PO Box 69, Clavet, SK, SOK OYO, Canada
lisaslilies@aol. com
www. lisaslily garden.com

LILIES LILIES
PO Box 17, Site 3, RR#1, Rocky Mountain House, AB, T4T 2A1, Canada
fax (403) 729-3221
LiliesLilies@telusplanet.net
www.telusplanet.net/public/mgshol/home.html

THE LILY NOOK
PO Box 846, Neepawa, MB, ROJ 1HO, Canada
tel (204) 476-3225
fax (204) 476-5482
www.lilynook.mb.ca

McFAYDEN SEED CO. LTD
30 9th Street, Suite 200, Brandon, MB, R7A 6N4 Canada
tel (204) 725-7300
fax (204) 725-1888

PARKLAND PERENNIALS
PO Box 506, Bruderheim, AB, Canada
parklandperennials@canada.com

RIVERSIDE GARDENS
18 Pony Trail, Riverside Estates, SK, S7K 1A2, Canada
rivgardlilies@home.com
Supplies only within Canada

VALLEY K GREENHOUSES
RR#1, Edberg, AB, TOB 1JO, Canada
tel (780) 877-2547
fax (780) 877-2540
gardenho@valleyk.com
www.valleyk.com

United Kindom

BLOMS BULBS
Primrose Nurseries, Melchbourne, Beds. MK44 1ZZ, England, UK
tel 01234 709099
fax 01234 709799
chrisblom@blomsbulbs.com

www.blomsbulbs.com
Selection of species and cultivars

CELEBRATIONS NURSERY
Tony Parks, 19 Sycamore
Centre, Rotherham, S. Yorks.
S65 1EN, England, UK
tel 01709 76980
Wide selection, many Orientals

PAUL CHRISTIAN
PO Box 468, Wrexham LL13
9XR, Wales, UK
tel 01978 366399
fax 01978 266466
paul@rareplants. co.uk
http://rareplants. co.uk
Species only, some rare

P. DE JAGER AND SONS LTD.
Staplehurst Road, Marden,
Kent TN12 9BP, England, UK
tel 01622 831235
fax 01622 832416
PdeJag@aol.com
www.dejagerflowerbulbs.co.uk
Species and cultivars

WILFORD BULB CO. LTD
69/71 Main Street, East Leake,
Leics. LE12 6PF, England, UK
tel/fax 01509 852905 (Tony
Cross) *Species and cultivars,
strong in LAs*

New Zealand
DUNHAMPTON LILY FIELDS
Hoods Rd, RD 1, Mt Somers,
Ashburton, SI, NZ
Asiatics and Orientals

ENCHANTMENT LILIES
41 Torquay, Abbotsford,
Dunedin, SI, NZ *Some Asiatics*

HUNTINGDON LILIES
Linwald, Ashburton,
Canterbury, SI, NZ
McLaren's Trumpets

LILIES IN BLOOM
RD2, Takaka, SI, NZ
tel 64-3-525-8353
info@bloom.co.nz
wwww. bloom.co.nz

LILIES INTERNATIONAL LTD
Fairfield Road, Levin, NI, NZ

tel/fax 64-6-368-5819
*Hybridizers, wholesale Asiatics,
Orientals*

LILIES UNLIMITED
88 Ngaroto Road, PO Box 300,
Te Awamutu, NI, NZ
tel 64-7-871-7588

WESTHURST GARDEN
NURSERY
52 Old West Coast Road, No. 6
RD, Christchurch, SI, NZ
tel (03) 342-9545
Canterbury Hybrid Trumpets

Australia
THE AUSTRALIAN LILIUM
SOCIETY
PO Box 208, Monbulk,
Victoria 3793, Australia
will provide suppliers

*Suppliers of cultures for
tissue and embryo*

United States
CAROLINA BIOLOGICAL
SUPPLY CO.
2700 York Road, Burlington,
NC 27215

GIBCO
519 Aldo Ave.
Santa Clara, CA 95050

SIGMA CHEMICAL CO.
PO Box 14508
St. Louis, MO 63178

VWR SCIENTIFIC
PO Box 3551
Seattle, WA 98124

United Kingdom
CHEMPAC
Garden Direct, Geddings
Road, Hoddesdon, Herts EN11
0LR Electromail PO Box 33,
Corby, Northants NN17 9EL,
UK
01992 890550

TETRA
Lambert Court, Chestnut
Avenue, Eastleigh, Hants SO53

3ZQ, UK
02380 620500

THERMOFORCE LTD
Wakefield Road, Cockermouth,
Cumbria CA13 0HS, UK
01900 823231

Lily societies

United States
NORTH AMERICAN LILY
SOCIETY
www.lilies.org
Publications, shows, seed

Canada
ALBERTA REGIONAL LILY
SOCIETY
www.tigerlily.ca/arls

CANADIAN PRAIRIES
mlily@sk.sympatico.ca

MANITOBA REGIONAL LILY
SOCIETY
www.manitobalilies.ca

ONTARIO REGIONAL LILY
SOCIETY
schieman@hotmail.com

S. SASK. LILY SOCIETY
www.ss/s.ca

North American readers, and
indeed most enthusiasts, will
find interesting information at:
pine.usask.ca/cofa/department
s/hort/hortinfo/misc/ whose
topics include lilies.

England
THE ROYAL HORTICULTURAL
SOCIETY (RHS) LILY GROUP
Produces annual *Lilies and
Related Plants* plus periodic
newsletters. Arranges visits to
gardens of interest. Many join
group to receive the extensive
co-operative seed list.

Australia
THE AUSTRALIAN LILIUM
SOCIETY
Branches in all main parts

New Zealand
AUCKLAND LILY SOCIETY

NZ LILY SOCIETY
PO Box 1394, Christchurch,
SI, NZ

OTAGO LILY SOCIETY

South Africa
SOUTH AFRICAN LILY
SOCIETY

Web sites
ROYAL HORTICULTURAL
SOCIETY
www.rhs.org.uk

RHS ADVISORY SERVICE
tel 01483 224234
www.rhs.org.uk/science/mn-
advisory-service.asp

RHS LILY GROUP
www.rhslilygroup.org

NORTH AMERICAN LILY
SOCIETY
www. lilies.org/

Literature

Fox, Derek, *Growing Lilies*,
Christopher Helm, 1985.

Jefferson-Brown, Michael,*The
Lily*, David & Charles, 1988.

Jefferson-Brown, Michael, *The
Gardener's Guide to Growing Lilies*,
David & Charles, 1995.

Jefferson-Brown, Michael,
Lilies, RHS/Cassell Wisley
Guide, 2002.

McRae, Edward Austin, *Lilies*,
Timber Press, 1998.

Synge, P. M., *Lilies*, Batsford,
1980.

Woodcock, H.B.D. and Stearn,
W. T., *Lilies of the World*, Country
Life, 1950.

Lily Yearbooks of the North
American Lily Society.

Key names

No attempt has been made in
this book to detail all the key
individuals involved in lily
culture, but you are likely to
come across the following:

BILL DOREEN The
mainspring of International
Lilies in New Zealand,
specialists in Oriental lilies.
Introduced 'Casa Blanca'.

JUDITH FREEMAN Runs the
Lily Garden in Vancouver and
has been responsible for much
scientific and technological
research into lily breeding.

VICKI MATTHEWS The
registrar for the lily genus,
based at the RHS Gardens,
Wisley, England, UK.
Supplements to the main
register are published to keep
information up to date. There
are still too many lilies that
have not been registered.
Those contemplating naming a
new cultivar can obtain a form
from the registrar.

EDWARD MCRAE After
training at the Royal Botanic
Garden in Edinburgh,
Scotland, joined the Jan de
Graaff team at the Oregon
Bulb Farms. Now a leading
breeder and authority.

PETER SCHENK Director of
breeding and research with
Bischoff Tulleken Lelies BV in
Holland. Has pioneered much
of the huge wave of breeding
and technology.

The details included here are
correct at the time of going to
press, but the publishers take
no responsibility for future
changes in website addresses
or telephone numbers.

index

Author's acknowledgments

Many people should be thanked for their contribution to this book. Jane O' Shea of Quadrille and Susanne Mitchell of the RHS conceived and nurtured the idea of the book, and Carole McGlynn was its dedicated midwife and editor. Paul Welti has been responsible for the book's elegant design. Andrew Lawson spent much of one summer season photographing lily species and cultivars as they opened, while Sarah Cuttle took all the practical shots. The majority of flowers were photographed in the author's garden, but others were shot in the splendid woodland garden of the successful enthusiast Tim Whiteley, where many species grow better than in their native stations. John Berkeley kindly allowed free access to the gardens at Spetchley Park outside Worcester, England, where *L. martagon* and *L. monadelphum,* in particular, run riot. Ron Blom of Bloms Bulbs donated bulbs of a large number of cultivars so that they could be grown on for photographing, and Tony Cross and his wife gave glorious cut flowers from their Chelsea Flower Show exhibits to provide important lily portraits. Dr. Alan Leslie, the former lily registrar at Wisley, has courteously answered all my queries about parentage and dates of introduction.

Photo acknowledgments

The publishers thank those who have contributed photographs to this book. All photographs are by Andrew Lawson except those by Sarah Cuttle (pages: 16; 19 top left, top right, top center; 66; 100; 112; 124; 128–29; 133; 136-37; 142; 143; 146–47; 149 top left, top center; 151) and Michael Jefferson-Brown (pages: 19 below right; 31 below left; 62; 64; 70–71; 82; 85–86; 92; 97 below left; 110 top left). Those on pages 10 and 11 © Lindley Library, The Royal Horticultural Society.